Centennial Journal
Sketches from the Coast

Maria Jane Schuyler Hatch

Transcribed by Terry Totten

Russian Hill Press Book
United States • United Kingdom • Australia

R̶H̶P̶ Russian Hill Press

The publisher is not responsible for websites or their content that are not owned by the publisher.

ISBN: 9798987928509 (softcover)
ISBN: 9798987928516 (eBook)

Library of Congress Control Number: 2023904678

Cover by Dragon Wing Publishing

Poem courtesy of Linda Hogan, Native American writer

To my mother, Virginia L. Lynch,
whose love, support, compassion and wisdom
made all the difference.

Walking, I am listening to a deeper way.
Suddenly all my ancestors are behind me.
Be still they say.
Watch and listen.
You are the result of the love of thousands.

Linda Hogan
Native American writer

Whispers in the wind
Of those from long ago
Guiding us with grace
That we might pass it on

Terry Totten

Introduction

Maria Jane Schuyler Hatch was my maternal great grandmother. She wrote her "Centennial Journal" in 1876 for her best friend, Clara Shelley. Clara did the same. At the end of the year they traded diaries for the next year and read each others' day by day. After Maria's was returned, she wrote again in 1878.

Maria specifically stated that her personal thoughts were for her dear and trusted friend's eyes only. I ask her forgiveness in sharing something so personal but felt compelled to do so because of its rich story and historical value.

Maria was born January 20, 1850 in or near Atlanta, Georgia. According to my grandmother, she was a "French scholar." She played the organ, piano and guitar and was an accomplished singer.

In the 1870s, Half Moon Bay was a small community on the California coast. Maria moved from Georgia to join her father, James Schuyler and her stepmother who owned the town's one and only hotel, the elegant Schuyler Hotel.

At that time, Rufus Hatch was co-owner of the Borden and Hatch sawmill in Purissima Canyon, south of Half Moon Bay. Family legend says that he fell in love with Maria at first sight. It was improper to introduce himself to a young lady, so he enrolled in piano lessons given by her. The plan worked and they were married on March 18, 1875. Rufus was 45, Maria was 25.

Each entry is filled with images of Maria's daily life. Some were of sorrow and heartbreak while most were filled with humor and fun. Faith was a very important part of her life, which no doubt, was a great comfort to her and her family as she died of tuberculosis in 1888, at the age of 38. She left behind her husband and four small children.

Maria was an adventurous, independent woman full of spunk and spirit.

I hope her inspiring words touch your heart as they have mine.

Family & Friends

Myra, Maria Jane Schuyler Hatch, pronounced "Mariah" Jane "Skyler" Hatch. 1850-1888

Ruf, Rufus Harvey Hatch, Maria's husband. 1829-1906

Ma, Phebe Jane Allen. Maria's stepmother. Second wife of James Schuyler. 1832-1912

Father, James Monroe Schuyler. Owner of The Schuyler Hotel where Maria lived for many years. 1812-1898

Lil, Mary Elizabeth Schuyler, Maria's sister, 1847-1905

Wesley, James Wesley Schuyler, Maria's brother. 1840-1910

Ellen, Ellen Elizabeth Donovan, wife of Wesley, mother of nine children. 1851-1917

Mary Jane Decker, Maria's mother. Died when Maria was two. 1829-1852

Clara M. Shelley, Maria's best friend who lived in Redwood City, California. 1849-1930

Local History

Amsport Landing is now Miramar.
The Woods refer to Purissima Canyon.
Half Moon Bay was originally named San Benito and then Spanishtown.

1876

Half Moon Bay
1876

Jan 1st

Dear Elva according
to agreement I commence my Journal,
but I am not satisfied with the book, for
the paper is very poor indeed but the
best I could get in this town over the
mountain, I begin the New Year in
a sleepy way for I was up attending a
party last night and in fact till four
Oclock this morning; which accounts
for my lack of brightness today, we
had quite a number of friends here
and passed the time pleasantly,
games of all kinds being the feature of
the evening; at twelve the bells were
rung and made quite a noise, the
Catholic bell for Midnight Mass continued
to ring long after the others ceased ringing
the citizens of this place bought a
quantity of powder and intended to
have a large cannon fired but the rain
prevented them from doing so,
A Ball was given at Pacific Hall and was
kept up till three Oclock this morning;
The Brass Band favored us with some
of their choicest selections, they stood
on the corners of the two principal streets
and blew as if their lives depended on the
music; I enjoyed all these things of course
but believe I liked the Turkey dinner
at noon about as much as I did the
other especially when we finished up with
a piece of Mrs's genuine Mince pie made
for the occasion. the afternoon being spent in
dreamland I will not tell about.

Half Moon Bay
January 1, 1876

Dear Clara,

According to agreement, I commence my journal but am not satisfied with the book for the paper is very poor indeed but the best I could get in this town over the mountain. I begin the New Year in a sleepy way for I was up attending a party last night and in fact until four o'clock this morning which accounts for my lack of brightness today. We had quite a number of friends here and passed the time pleasantly. Games being the featured of the evening. At twelve the bells were rung and made quite a noise. The Catholic bell for midnight mass continued to ring long after the others ceased ringing. The citizens of this place bought a quantity of powder and intended to have a large cannon fired but the rain prevented them from doing so.

A ball was given at Pacific Hall and was kept up till three o'clock this morning. The brass band favored us with some of their choicest selections. They stood on the corner of the two principal streets and blew as if their lives depended on the music. I enjoyed all these things of course but believe I liked the turkey dinner at noon about as much as I did the others especially when we finished with a piece of Ma's genuine mince pie, made for the occasion. Later, the afternoon being spent in dreamland I will not tell about.

January 2, 1876

Welcome sweet day of rest. I wanted to go to church this morning but it began to rain almost directly after breakfast and as I was afraid to sit still during services with my feet wet, I thought it would not be prudent to go, but if the weather breaks, we will all go this evening. Mr. Hazzard, the new minister, is much liked by his congregation for the interest he seems to take in preparing his sermons, which do not seem long enough for his hearers because they are so interesting. Lil is reading the Evangel, Father is also reading, Ma is preparing to do so and Ruf is looking at me write. I have been anxiously looking for a letter from Clara today and I was a little disappointed when I inquired and found "no letter" the answer but I suppose she is busy preparing to return home after her pleasant visit at Oakland.

Being Sunday and rainy it is an unusually dull day on the streets and a great many left here today who had been visiting their friends till after the holidays so it seems lonesome to most everyone. I cannot find much to write now and Ma offers me a nice orange, the delicious flavor of which I can almost taste so I will close and eat it. If you were here I might give you a suck on the peeling of it for at times I am most generous.

January 3, 1876

Rain in the morning, rain at noon and still rain to greet us in the evening. I declare it makes me feel as blue as indigo and as stupid as an idiot. I believe Stockton will be a fit place for us all if this weather continues. Just as I am writing it begins to hail like sixty. O' wouldn't I like to see a glorious snow storm and have a sleigh ride as they do East this time of year. I have been busy all the morning mending a coat for Ruf. It was a real job as both the armholes were torn and the lining of the sleeves worn out. This afternoon I made my riding skirt into an evening dress and trimmed it with black alpaca braid. It looks very neat and as the cloth was wide, it was easy to cut over. Ma is practicing her music lesson, "Tripping through the Meadows." It is so pretty, I never tire listening to it. Wesley has just finished putting a stove up in the parlor, it is a real beauty called "Onward." Lil is sewing beside me and wants to know how much nonsense I intend to put down here. We think of playing a game of dominoes this eve unless company should come in and prevent. We have fun for sometimes we set an orange or apple on the table and say, "It will belong to the one who wins the game." Then we take so much pains to keep the double six out!

January 4, 1876

Well for a wonder the rain has stopped and the sun shines. It is a welcome sight to everyone. Ruf and Father will soon start on their journey south and I would be sorry to have it rain and the sea rough while they were on the water. Ruf wants me to go with him but I had my share a few weeks ago. I went to Goat Island to take Anna home. Her father met us at Oakland and took us in a row boat to the island. The bay was rough. I was seasick and I had enough of sailing for one year at least. The next day we came over to Oakland and went onboard the ship, "Three Brothers." It is next in size to the, "Great Eastern" and was so heavy laden with coal, lumber etc. that we were obliged to have a tug rescue take her to the San Francisco harbor to finish loading as the water was deeper there. Although this did not happen today and is not in journal form, I thought it might be as interesting to you as it was to me, for I felt I had done some grand thing after I got off the ship.

I spent the afternoon with Maria Levy and found the time to pass pleasantly. Received a postal card from cousin Robert today wishing me a Merry Christmas and Happy New Year, it came a little late but was sent from New York.

My little Beauty is singing very sweet in the hall. He had a cold and I gave him some medicine and now he is much better, birds are so much company.

January 5, 1876

Beautiful sunshine today. I will take a ride if Ruf can spare the time to drive. The horses have been idle so long, he is almost afraid to let me manage them and the roads are very muddy yet. I have almost made up my mind to walk down to the beach if he does not take me to ride. I might fall in a puddle or two but it would not hurt me much. We all went to a temperance lecture at the church. It was delivered by a reformed Jew. We found the lecture about the same as such generally are and all might have passed off straight enough had not a man who was intoxicated come in. He made a very polite bow to the congregation then seated himself and then he felt he would like to make a reply to the lecturer. That set a party of girls giggling in the back seats and the sexton was obliged to take him by the shoulder and show him where the door was. As he was going down the aisle he said, "Young ladies, good night."

Wesley says he will come upstairs this evening and help us sing. He has a very fine bass voice and we like to have him sing with us. Lil and I have been learning "The Hunter's Song." She sings soprano and I take the alto although my voice is hardly heavy enough.

January 6, 1876

Yes, this is Thursday and I will give Lil a lesson on the piano if she knows her other lesson. The wind blows very hard and we are almost afraid to make fire for fear of setting the chimney on fire. Sent an order to Sherman and Hyde for some new music; a march and some nocturnes for piano and a song with accompaniment for guitar.

Ma gave me a book called, "Life of Livingstone," and I enjoyed reading it very much. The engravings are also fine. Dr. McCurdy lent us some books to look at called "Picturesque America." It is published in numbers and is fifty cents per number. The whole book contains twenty four numbers I believe. It is printed on buff tinted paper and is quite a large paged book. Mr. and Mrs. Levy are coming in the parlor this evening to play a very laughable game of "Snap." It is amusing to hear all at once crying "Snap!" Some of the pictures are almost alike and it puzzles us so to tell them from others that we get caught and have to pay a forfeit every time we make a mistake.

January 7, 1876

Rain again and windy enough to blow the head off of any man, woman or child who happens to be on the streets. There is a perfect little creek running by the front of the hotel and lots of mud to make mud pies with. I expected Ellen Johnston to spend the day with me but the weather has prevented her from coming out as it is quite a distance from her house to here! How provoking it is. Father is sitting next to me and some how touched me and my pen fell right on the book of course so you will have to excuse as it was not done carelessly. There are two little boys about eight years of age fighting in front of my window and a lot of men stand cheering them on. I think it is a shame and I feel like telling those men to go about their business and also separate the boys and tell them how wrong it is to fight.

The flag staff fell from the top of the Odd Fellows Hall last night and the top was broken. A young French girl stopped here today on her way from

Pescadero to San Mateo. She had been on the pebble beach during the rain and had collected a quantity of beautiful pebbles and a number of shells. She intends to return East next week and take her treasures with her. It must have been a very unpleasant trip in the storm and a leaky stage coach.

January 8, 1876

Saturday is generally considered a busy day for most people but I have but little to do so I think of making a worsted mat, pink and white.

The Odd Fellows are to install their officers this evening and Father is to be Vice Grand of the Lodge. Mr. Scoffield came over on the stage today to attend the Installation.

The weather is pleasant today but not very much sunshine gladdens our hearts. Received a Postal card from Clara Shelly today stating that she had returned to Redwood City.

Saw Clarence Merrill, he was on his way to Pescadero to work on a ranch there. He says Arthur is there too. I have a paper of fresh chocolate candy. How would you like a bite?

The Grangers are to meet in The Good Templar's Hall the first Saturday of each month. I forgot all about it last week and I ought to have gone. I have taken two degrees and have two more to take before I can become a member. Ruf has been a member for some time and I must hurry up and get through before the next Granger picnic.

A new cook came out here yesterday and father

discharged the other one, so, we had an extra dinner today. A new broom sweeps clean so we do not know how long it will last.

January 9, 1876

I must tell you all about the Odd Fellows supper last night. As Father was to be installed Vice Grand. Ma thought she would give him a little surprise so she got a nice oyster supper and invited the Odd Fellows to come over. There were twenty two of them and they seemed to enjoy their supper very much. They had mince and cranberry pie and several kinds of cake. When all had finished eating, Father treated each to a cigar. Then the Grand Master of the Lodge was called upon for a speech. He made a very laughable speech about Odd Fellow's wives and Judge Ames got up and spoke about organizing a "Sister of Rebekah," Lodge, and as Ma belongs to the Order in San Francisco she will know how to manage affairs.

Lil and I went to Church this morning and heard a very good sermon about denominations. He said there were no Baptists in Heaven, no Methodists in Heaven, no Catholics there but all Christians were there. He says if we are Christians the denomination has nothing to do with it. We are going this evening to hear Dr. McCurdy lecture of temperance, liquor, it's evil effects on the brain and nerves. The weather is pleasant but cold and everybody doubled up with the cold.

Supper is now ready and I wish you were here to help me eat it.

January 10, 1876

Weather pleasant and shiny, but the people are all sad for a very nice woman died last night. She has six children and was deserted by her husband a short time ago. Last night she brought into the world a sweet little baby girl and an hour afterward breathed her last. Her poor little children were left alone in the world. Ruf wanted to take one of the boys but as they are Catholics the Priest will not allow them to go into Protestant families so I suppose most of them will be sent to the Orphan Asylum.

Mrs. Nichols came to see us this afternoon and invited us to a quilting party at her house next week and I think we will have a pleasant time.

January 11, 1876

We have all been sewing on a dress for Lil she wanted to get it finished today. I went to see Fannie Freitas but she had gone with a party of young folks down to the beach to get clams and I did not see her, so I spent the afternoon with Mrs. Kelly and had a very pleasant time. Her baby has grown very fast. Mr. and Mrs. Lewis are going to a lecture this evening and if Ruf is too tired to go I will go with them. Ruf has been away all day on horseback and as he is not used to riding it will tire him a good deal.

January 12, 1876

Weather cold and windy. Gave a music lesson this morning and about ten o'clock Ruf drove up to the door with the buggy and horses and wanted me to go with him for a ride, so, we went as far as Mrs. James Deniston's, saw her daughter, Amelia. Spent two hours with them and drove back. The ride along the beach was cold and the roads very muddy and we were obliged to walk our horses most of the way home. In the afternoon Ellen Johnston, Maria Levy, Fannie Stegman and Mrs. Gareline came to see us. Mrs G had a young baby with her and could not stay long, but the other three stayed all the afternoon and took supper with us. We had a splendid time playing "Authors" and "Snap," then we looked at some new steroscopic views Ma has, played piano, sang songs, then stopped and had a good long talk together. Ellen wanted to go to a Committee meeting at the church to arrange the time for a S.S.[1] Concert so we all walked with her and afterward went to McAmes gate with Fannie Stegman and now I must go and pack a valise for Father and Ruf to take with them on their trip and must see if I can help Lil get a key for her satchel.

January 13, 1876

Pleasant day. The ocean is as calm as it possibly can be. I am glad it is for the folk started today for the city and sail on Saturday for Los Angeles. Lil went to Belmont too and Ma and I feel dreadful lonely now.

---

[1] SS no doubt stands for Sunday school.

They will be gone near two weeks and it will seem so long to us. We wanted them to go but when the time came for them to start we hated to have them go, but they will have a nice time I guess.

Lil will stay a couple of days at Belmont and then go to Redwood to see Clara. Ma and I will spend this evening with Mrs Lewis for we won't hardly know what to do with ourselves.

January 14, 1876

Ma and I took a nice walk right after breakfast. It was a pleasant morning and we were afraid the wind would blow in the afternoon. We sat on the beach sand near an hour and watched the waves roll in and the spray fly. There were plenty of whitecaps. We ate oranges and coconut candy, then walked home and had a good appetite for our dinner. Mrs. Metzgar came to see us this afternoon and spent a couple of hours. Ellen and Hannah Johnston came and invited me to a singing bee at their father's house this evening, they have invited quite a number and anticipate a good time.

January 15, 1876

An old friend of Ma's came on the stage. She lost her husband three months ago and was married again yesterday to a man much younger than herself. Was that not a very wicked thing to do? Her other husband had always been kind to her and to think she could forget him so soon. She is on her way to Purissima to stay a few days. Ma has run over to the store to get some muslin to make Father's shirts and I will go out into the garden and get some chickweed for the birds. So I will finish writing this evening.

Took a walk over the long bridge as the day was so pleasant. When it was time for the steamer to pass, we raised a flag on the hotel. Ma and I went on the upper piazza and looked through the glasses at the vessel. It seemed further out at sea than usual. The ocean is so calm, they will have a good time.

January 16, 1876

Went to church this morning. Sermon was St. Luke Vl chap 4 1st verse. We had quite a large congregation for this place. The pleasant weather continues. Mary David came and took supper with me, then we went to church with ma this evening, the text was from Revelations last chapter 17th verse. The spirit and the bride say: Come!

January 17, 1876

Weather fine and roads good. I went to visit a friend but found her house empty. She had gone to ride. Mr. Levy came very near setting our house on fire last evening. He made up a large fire in the fireplace using light wood and putting coal oil on to make it roar. It made a great cracking tune, sparks flew above the house and frightened us badly. Ma had a severe headache and she got so scared that her headache disappeared. They finally put the fire out but the chimney had a good warming up. Ma and I have been playing a game of "checkers" this evening and she got more kings every time than I.

January 18, 1876

We went to see Mrs. Ames this afternoon, she gave me a cabinet picture[2] of her little boy. We enjoyed our visit there very much for she has a large cabinet filled with curiosities from Yosemite Valley and other places in California also minerals from other parts of the world. Petrified wood from the Petrified Forest. Pinecones from Calavaras Big Trees. She has her cabinet carpeted with fresh green moss just gathered as we are in visiting fancy we will spend the evening with Mrs. Davids, the wife of Mr. Hatch's partner in the blacksmith shop. Got a letter from Lil today. She says she is enjoying herself with Clara.

January 19, 1876

I see by the "Call" the steamer "Orizaba" has arrived at Wilmington so Father and Ruf will have a few miles to travel by rail before they reach Los Angeles. I am making some clover-leaf tatting for an apron and Ma is sewing tape trimming. Last evening

---

[2] Cabinet picture or photograph or cabinet card was a style of photography which was widely used for photographic portraiture after 1870.

we ate a piece of lemon pie and neither of us were able to sleep well. Received a letter from Cousin Mary, Seneca Falls, N.Y. She says the moss work I sent arrived safe. Looks like rain today, went to see Cora Levie. I must practice a little this evening for I am sadly neglecting my music.

January 20, 1876

Cold, colder, coldest. The mountains are covered with snow and our streets are filled with hail. It makes me shiver to lookout the window!

Today is my birthday. Ma always gives me a book, but as the roads were too muddy to travel, she has not been to the city and could not get one. Mary Davids gave me two very pretty mats- blue and white worsted and a cabinet photograph of herself. I consider that a nice present. Ruf is away from home, most likely he will forget all about my birthday. I must write a letter to Matilda Harris in San Mateo and post it before stage time.

January 21, 1876

I declare we are having a genuine snow-storm. How pretty the flashes look coming down and the ground is so white and pretty. It is rather pleasant to sit by a bright fire and watch the streets, but to be out and nearly freeze would be a different view of the matter. Just wrote two letters, one to San Francisco and one to Buchanan, Mich. Received one from Clara wishing me a happy birthday and telling me about some coconut candy she and Lil have been making. She was mean to tell me for she knew it would make me want a bite. Mr. and Mrs. Hartley have just returned from a visit of three weeks in the city.

January 22, 1876

More snow, hail and rain, mud, water and slop. I went out to buy some buttons for my shoes and came back with mud enough to make a pie sticking to my rubbers.

Received a dispatch from Ruf. He sent it from Los Angeles. They are to come back on the steamer "Mohongo" which will leave tomorrow. Received a Postal Card from San Francisco. Ma is sewing on the machine, making a skirt and the four canaries are singing at the top of their voices, they always do when I play the piano too.

January 23, 1876

I think if this place keeps dull much longer I will have to fill my journal leaves as Mark Twain did his. One whole page consisted of, "Got up, washed, went to bed." And he must have been in some enterprising town like this I should judge.

We are having a terrible storm and the wind is blowing a perfect gale. The ocean is very rough. Waves are dashing against the shore in a fearful manner. Trees are blowing down and the house shakes as a cradle would rock. Fannie Freitas got so lonesome she came over here to spend the afternoon and we were glad to have her for it. Stormed so hard we could not go to church, there will be no service this evening on account of the weather.

January 24, 1876

More storm and wind. We are having a terrible winter equal to the winter of 1862 I think. The road from Pescadero here is impassable. Bridges washed away and slides on the mountains. The stage from San Mateo was obliged to take the passengers back to town as there was a part of the road washed away and they came very near having an accident. Mr. Taft brought the mail over on horseback. Mr. and Mrs. Lewis spent the evening with us.

January 25, 1876

The wind died away about midnight so this morning is very pleasant. The sun arose in its' glory as if it always wore just such a smiling face instead of tears falling in torrents. Early this morning we saw a beautiful rainbow and almost everybody was out admiring it. Ma and I went to the store to get some cloth to make Father a comfortable riding coat. She intends to line it with light blue, his favorite color and will give it to him for a surprise. The "Senator" sailed this morning from San Francisco and she seemed to glide along nicely in the water.

Today is Chinese New Year and they are celebrating it by setting off great packages of fire crackers and firing guns. All the children in the neighborhood are gathered around to pick up stray firecrackers and the Chinamen are running from one wash house to another greeting each other after the American fashion on Christmas and New Year.

The lady who rented our house at the saw mill had a baby on the 23rd, a girl. Everybody had a cold and sore throat around here, we expect Lil home today. Belle and Fannie Nichols came to see us this afternoon. Carrie Shourds came this evening to borrow Ma's Scrap Book. She wants to select a piece of poetry suitable for a concert and there are a great many pretty pieces in the book.

January 26, 1876

A pleasant morning but it looks as if it was trying hard to rake up a shower or two before noon.

The body of a man was found on the beach at the foot of our street. It is supposed to be the body of a Spaniard who was drowned about a week ago. Several fisherman were out in a small boat and it capsized throwing them to the mercy of the waves. The poor fellow was not seen by the rest and it is supposed as soon as he reached the water he was grabbed by a shark or some similar fish for when they found him, every particle of flesh was eaten off leaving a terrible sight. He had one boot on by which his friends identified him. He was buried on the beach just above high water mark, and as he was Catholic, the bell has been tolling sadly.

Received a letter from Anna Francis. She is at Oakland School and allowed to go home but once a month. She wants to see me very much. She says I wonder if she could speak "Miss Skinner" and make it as laughable for you and I as she did that evening. Saw Mrs. Cooper this morning. Received two letters, one from Pescadero and one from Salt Lake City. I wanted to see how smart I could be so I tried to make 1/2 yard of double tatting this afternoon, found I was not half as smart as I thought I was for I came short quite a piece.

January 27, 1876

Weather pleasant, light showers during the forenoon. Went down the street to buy some dates and figs, but could not find so had to be satisfied with prunes and Brazil nuts.

Received a letter from San Francisco and Peterson's Magazine.

Ellen Johnson came to make me a present of two very nice mats, pink and white for the piano. She intended them for my birthday but it stormed so she could not come down. Ma says I ought to feel quite matted this year for I got two pairs of mats.

We saw the steamer "Ancon"[3] pass this afternoon about four o'clock and raised our flag again as the folks did not come on the "Mohongo" they were surely on this boat. They were quite near land.

---

[3] The Ancon: an ocean-going wooden sidewheel steamship built in San Francisco in 1867. She carried both passengers and freight. Later in her career, she began coastal runs between San Diego and San Francisco.

January 28, 1876

Nice weather. Mrs. Lea and Mrs. Hartley spent the afternoon with us. I went to stay awhile with Mrs. Metzgar. She was taken suddenly ill with pleurisy. She was suffering very much and hardly able to speak without screeching. Received a letter from my uncle in New York. He says there was a grand time there on New Year's Eve. All the cannons and guns in the place had to be fired and there was a great danger of accidents.

The banjo is making such a noise downstairs that I can hardly tell what I am writing!

January 29, 1876

Got up and took a nice walk before breakfast, it was a very pleasant sunrise and although the streets are muddy it was a change from sitting in the house all day.

Lil came home on the noon stage and said she got badly frightened on the summit for the stage leaned over on one side so far it came near being upset. The passengers had to get out and walk quite a distance.

Alice Selleck and Lizzie were here waiting for the stage. We are to spend the evening next door and have a game of dominoes.

I was invited out to a certain lady's house in this town to stay all afternoon, to dinner and spend the evening. There were about one dozen young folks and they had two packs of these common cards such as are used in barrooms. They wished me to join them but I could not. I think such pastime fascinates young men and they think if girls will play it is all right, but just wait a little. Some evening when it is not convenient for their sisters to play with them, they will be off to the saloon to spend their time. Their plea is "It is no more harm to handle cards in a saloon than in a parlor," and they are about right. They use the self same kind but it leads them to drink for they will play for whiskey I have always been taught to detest the sight of cards and my father can say he never played a game in his life. He doesn't know how.

January 30, 1876

Went to church this morning. The text was St. Luke 24th chapter 48th verse "Ye are witnesses of these things." Mr. Hazzard gave us quite a lengthy discourse. We were caught in the rain coming home but walked as fast as we could. Ma is reading, Lil is looking out of the window and I have my own work at present to attend to, my journal writing. Ma calls it my "Daily list of fibs" but you know it cannot be so from me who is so honest.

Albert Masterson, a young boy who used to live with us years ago, came to see us today. He had not a cent of money and walked all the way from San Francisco here, about twenty four miles. He was very tired and happy when he got to the Hotel. We were all glad to see him and will do all we can for him.

The fog is so heavy we can scarcely see across the street. Wesley calls it a "Scotch mist from Ireland."

January 31, 1876

I must tell you what a pleasant time we had last evening. Mr. Chase Jr. from Santa Cruz was here and as his uncle is an old friend of Father's we were pleased to have him visit us. After church was over he came upstairs with us and we had such a nice time singing hymns. Dr. McGurdy and Mr. Joe Levy came up as soon as we commenced singing and Wesley also came to sing bass with us. Those who were not in the room said it sounded first rate.

February 1, 1876

A delightful day on both land and sea. We received a telegraph dispatch that Father and Rufus were in San Francisco and will be home tomorrow noon. Lil and I went to carry a pitcher of soup to Mrs. Metzger as she is not yet well enough to eat much.

I am to have my Wheeler and Wilson brought down from the mill for I have quite a number of things I want to make and can do them so much better on the machine. Tucks are very tedious to do by hand. I must now practice my "Lady of the Castle."

I have been sewing on a night gown and Ma says she will run them on the machine.

February 2, 1876

Father and Ruf came home today. They were glad to get back after being away three weeks. They brought us a couple dozen oranges from Los Angeles. They rode right under orange trees on the roadside. They bought some land at Santa Monica with a house on it.

Martha (Ruf's niece) sent me a beautiful tidy in crochet and sent Ma a pair of mats, white with blue border. Father brought Ma a set of earrings and a breast pin and Lil a set of earrings very pretty. Father and Ma took a buggy ride this afternoon. Margie Walker called this evening.

February 3, 1876

Windy and very unpleasant. Took a walk as far as the stable to see the horses. Father was exercising Lady Alzerine and Prince. Ruf took me to ride as far as Purissima this afternoon. We called to see Grace MeGinty on our way back. Lil and Mrs. Lewis went to the beach with a party and had quite a pleasant time. One buggy had upset on the side of the road but no one got hurt. Mr. Kelly's chimney caught fire this morning but was put out before it did any harm.

February 4, 1876

Amy Sexton and I went to take a walk around the school house and part way to the beach. We got back about ten o'clock. I then gave a music lesson "Fredonia March," ate dinner, went to the Post Office, got a Postal Card and a letter from a lady in Panamint. She says the snow is five inches deep and water freezes in a pitcher in her sitting room even when they keep a big fire till ten o'clock at night. She said they have a glorious time sliding down hills. Lil and I went out to make calls this afternoon. We had a nice time, on our way back we were joined by Jeannetta Johnston who came home with us. I went up to the stable and watched Father train Henry Miller, his favorite horse. He will come to Father whenever he snaps his whip at him.

February 5, 1876

Ruf went to the Free Mason's Lodge last evening. Wesley's wife and children came home on the noon stage. Little Phebe looks so tall; we have not seen her for about two months. Everett begins to talk.

Ruf and I went to see old Mrs. Bailey. She intends to go home to Santa Barbara tomorrow and we wanted to see her before she started. She is about ninety seven or eight years old, smokes a pipe and dresses in old style. She is a very pleasant old lady, one that you could not help liking. We spent a very agreeable afternoon for a number of ladies and gentlemen called to bid goodbye to Mrs. Bailey.

Coming home, we almost turned the buggy over in a big mud hole. The side tipped up and we had hard work to balance it. The roads are in a fearful condition. As we came to Purissima we saw the ruins of the Hotel, nothing remained standing but the two chimneys. A few hours before, as we rode by, it was all right and the sign "Purissima House," looked as natural as ever. It seemed strange that in so short a time it should be burnt down. It caught fire from the parlor chimney, They were insured.

Ruf went to the 'Granger's Lodge.' I should have gone but felt too lazy. I have another degree to take before I can be called a member.

February 6, 1876

I did not attend church this morning, weather very fine. Abe Nichols came to sing some hymns with us. We all went to the S.S. Concert this evening. It was splendid. There were some very small children who sang and spoke pieces, one is Belle Knapp. She is four years old and so cunning. Hattie and Ella Stilson spoke a dialogue very well. Carrie Shourds spoke "The Three Travelers," which created quite a laugh. The whole school were dressed very prettily and sang a great many new songs. A small boy spoke a piece something about wanting the audience to come down with the mumps and then he passed the hat around and collected $16.85 cts. The school then sang a parting song. The minister closed the meeting and we came home well satisfied with our way of spending the Sabbath evening.

February 7, 1876

Got up, dressed, ate an orange, went up to the stable to meet Ruf who was feeding the horses, came back and rung the door bells of our neighbors on our way. Ate breakfast, gave my bird a bath, made fire in the sitting room, braided a piece of my blue silk apron, read a piece in "Santa Monica Outlook," spent half hour looking out the window to see papers fly in the wind, ate lunch, practiced, sewed rest of time and talked, ate supper, read evening paper, wrote my journal and now good night.

February 8, 1876

Rained all last night and blew a perfect hurricane, windows rattled and doors slammed so that many were unable to sleep. Today the wind has ceased somewhat but the rain still comes down in torrents and genuine rivers are formed in the streets. The ocean is very rough and angry, white caps are dashing against the shore. Gave Lil a music lesson called, "The Roub," a sort of Irish jig.

Spent the afternoon with Maria Levy and learned how to make the daisy mats. She was making a hair-pin box with a deer and fawn worked in blue worsted. I have started to make some gold colored silk tatting, and intend to put it on a sack of light blue merino. I must now wind up for Ma has promised me a pig's foot pickled for supper and I am very fond of trotters. Ruf says he knows I am writing fibs or stretching the truth but he had better look out for his lame ear. I might chew it again.

A dear little boy who lives near us was unfortunate enough to cut one of his fingers off in a hay cutter, His father brought him here immediately and the doctor fixed the hand as well as he could but could not sew the finger on as many supposed he might.

February 9, 1876

Cloudy and more rain, lightning last night and some thunder, spent the morning in Mrs. Hartley's room sewing and the afternoon with Mrs. Lewis next door.

Went to the candy store and bought some splendid broken candy that was just sent from the Palace Hotel Store and is delicious. I also got some coconut sticks nice and fresh. Valentines are now paraded in all the windows and are very comic looking. I expect to receive my share of them as I always do. I sent two way to New York and suppose I will get paid back for it from my cousins. Ruf made a nice frame for my worsted work.

February 10, 1876

Quite a pleasant day. Ma and I have just returned from the dry goods store. We bought some muslin and we found the streets very muddy but wore our rubbers to keep our feet dry. Fannie Stegman spent a couple of hours with us. She was telling us about a horseback ride she took a few days ago and as her horse was a pacer I guess she enjoyed her ride very much. Then I told of a ride I took on a trotting horse and how I had to fairly catch my breath. Mrs. Sexton is to spend the evening with us and we must have some pop-corn and apples. Got a letter from Los Angeles from Martha Jones. It came up in two days.

February 11, 1876

I do believe we are doomed to have one day of sunshine and six of shadow this winter for as soon as a pleasant day comes and everybody goes out-to-air themselves and see how their neighbors got along with their houses leaking and almost drowning them out, there is sure to be a heavier storm next day. This morning it started about daylight and now at 9 o'clock in the morning, it is still pouring as if the dust had not been laid for a year and we were anxious for a shower. Ellen gave me a very pretty pink silk necktie, latest-style and two fancy handkerchiefs braided with white linen and having lace on the edge.

February 12, 1876

Clear and cool. Etta Tilton, Jennie Dolloff and Mrs. Josie Morey came back on the noon stage as school will commence on Monday and two of them are teachers.

The schoolhouse has had another coat of paint and looks real pale. The desks are freshly varnished and the trustees want to raise money enough to buy some nice pictures for the first grade room.

I made a scarlet and white mat today to give to a girl. I should have made another for a pair but could not find any more worsted the color I wanted.

February 13, 1876

Sunday. Clear and bright. I think of all the days the Sabbath is the most gloomy if it rains, for then we cannot go to church and it is generally quiet indoors.

I will have to go on an errand of mercy this morning for a poor woman who has done my washing over a year is sick and is in need of aid. She has nothing in the house to eat but potatoes and does not relish them when sick, so I will take her some bread and soup. She has a husband who spends all the money he earns and all of her's that he can find for whiskey. They have four small children and are Catholics, but do not seem to find much help from their own Church. I have been asking my friends for old clothing and anything they could really spare. It is the same sad story, a drunkard for a husband and hungry children to feed.

Read in the Gazette of Mr. Winger's son a lad of 15 who was found in the field shot by accident with his own hand. Must get ready for evening service. Text was Hebrew 11th chap 23, 24, 25 verses a sermon on Moses. The church was quite full although the streets are very muddy and travel is very slow.

February 14, 1876

Pleasant weather. This is St. Valentine's Day and everybody is having fun sending and receiving valentines. The new style is quite pretty and although not at all fancy, is not insulting. I received two, Ruf two, Lil four and Wesley four very laughable ones. I sent a number of comic ones to others. One man in this town got a valentine from the City. It seems to be a very mean one for he made the remark that if he had known who the sender was, he would have shot him dead. Where a person sends such as that, it is no joking matter.

Went to see my wash woman and gave her money and bread. She seemed more comfortable than yesterday. Miss Morey came to take a music lesson but I did not give her any.

February 15, 1876

More nice weather. Mr. Nichols, an old gentleman of seventy eight years, died here yesterday and was buried today at two o'clock. He could not be kept over one night for he died of dropsy and they were obliged to part with his body sooner than they wished. Our family attended the funeral excepting myself. He was buried at Purissima. Spent the evening with my sister-in-law, got my hair trimmed and it looks real pretty in short curls. Ma and Ruf are playing checkers.

February 16, 1876

Clear and shiny. People begin to travel and the stages are full. I sent a telegraph dispatch to Lizzie Anderson telling her I would be in the city tomorrow evening so I suppose I will have to pack my trunk as I intend to stay over a week.

February 16, 1876
San Francisco (sic)

I am glad the weather is pleasant for I wish to ride on the outside of the stage. My trunk is now ready and I believe everything else for I hate to go off and forget half that I wanted to do. Ruf says he will get lonesome if I stay over three days, but I expect to have a good time. Ma is preparing for a masquerade ball supper to be given on Washington's Birthday and she is head over heels in work but won't let me help her. I must now get my dinner and be off.

Arrived safe. Met Lizzie at the depot watching every one who stepped off thinking it would be me. I had to see about my trunk and give the check to the baggage master; when Lizzie saw me she jumped about six feet, not up in the air but towards me. We took a car and were soon at her house No. 126 Capp St. near 17th. Her two children Harry and Minnie kissed me and said, "Oh, here is Aunt Ria." Lizzie their mother used to play together twelve years ago. (sic)

February 18, 1876

Lay awake a long time last night I suppose on account of being in a strange room. Got up early for the sun was shining brightly through the curtains. Had breakfast then got ready to go down town and do some shopping. Lizzie and I started about ten o'clock and did not get back till six. I had a number of articles to buy for ladies in Half Moon Bay who wanted them for the Masquerade. Then I bought a concertina instrument for a gentleman and sent them all out together by post. I had to get a moss picture framed and have several things stamped to embroider. I met May Donald and Fannie Rouse. Fannie says her mother and sister, Mary will start for Philadelphia next week to be gone a few months.

February 19, 1876

Captain Anderson got a carriage and took Lizzie and myself out to the new Park, it was a beautiful drive over the grounds. It seemed as if everybody and their friends were out and I guess it was because it was Saturday. There was a horse race on the track but we were none of us interested in it. Policeman were stationed in different parts of the Park to prevent fast driving. The wind commenced blowing about two o'clock and we started homeward.

The Captain drove through some of the finest streets of the city and I had a view of many beautiful residences. Among them were Sharon's, Ralston's, Fry's, Miller's and a great many whose names I cannot remember, but whose houses and grounds shall long be associated with my pleasant drive.

We arrived home and found supper on the table which did our eyes good for we were all hungry.

February 20, 1876

Sunday in the City with its' bells ringing so joyous and making such a sweet chime. We got up late as is generally the case on Sunday morning, had a late breakfast and then prepared for Church, but by the time Lizzie got herself ready and the two children washed and dressed we were too late for services. I was disappointed for I could have gone alone had I known the result of waiting. In the evening Captain Madison and daughter Lisa came and we had some nice singing for Lizzie sings soprano well and Lisa is strong Alto, I played the accompaniment.

February 21, 1876

As this is wash day and Lizzie wants to help her girl get through the work I will go to town alone. (Evening) Did quite a lot of walking today. Bought 10 yards of empress (ashes of roses) and two yards of pink alpaca for trimming. Took it to a lady on Third Street to have it cut and basted, bought a little doll for Minnie and a ruffled skirt for Phebe. Captain Anderson, Lizzie and myself went to the Market to buy turkey for dinner. They got a large, fat one, and some cranberries. I got weighed while there and weigh 126 pounds. We met Mrs. Cook and Mrs. Brown on the street.

February 22, 1876

Honor to Washington! Cannons, guns, and everything that can be fired off is proclaiming independence. Flags are floating and bells ringing. Boys shouting and girls singing. Soldiers parading and in fact, the Centennial year is showing itself, for today is equal to any fourth of July I ever saw. We all went to Woodward's Gardens[4] to spend the afternoon and settle our turkey dinner. We saw the baby camel

---

[4] Woodward's Gardens, commonly referred to as "The Gardens," was a combination amusement park, museum, art gallery, zoo, and aquarium operating from 1866 to 1891 in the Mission District of San Francisco.

and although but a couple of weeks old, it is so large it looks like a half grown horse. The mother was very proud of it even if it was ugly. I saw a number of new curiosities and birds that were not there a few months ago. We had a dish of ice cream and then went in to see the performance which lasted over an hour, singing and gymnastic exercises were the chief feature, skating took the floor after that.

February 23, 1876

I thought best to stay at home today as we had been out every other day. So, Lizzie and I cut out some sewing and we spent part of our time in sewing, another part in reading David Copperfield by Dickens and the rest of the time in playing piano. I have a new piece that is all the rage here called "Pretty as a Picture." It has some very nice chords in it and is a pleasing air. Mr. Moore a gentleman and neighbor spent the evening here. He is real jolly and kept us laughing most of the time with his jokes and Irish yarns. Then he wanted me to play a few jigs for him and it was as much as he could do to keep his seat. He said if I had not been a stranger to him he should have danced.

February 24, 1876

We went shopping again today and as we were too far from home to get back in time for lunch we went to Shain's Restaurant and got some oysters on the half shell and a cup of coffee. It tasted good for we were tired and hungry and got rested. I bought a china cup and saucer for Ma and intend to have Ma's birthday 1876, printed on it. It will not be finished for a few days as it will have to be burnt to keep the gilt from rubbing off.

February 25, 1876

Weather is quite gloomy today so we have a nice fire in the sitting room and are sewing. Lizzie is running the Grover and Baker sewing machine and I am braiding a brown linen apron for myself. The children are playing with pencil and paper and are very quiet, the music teacher is coming to give Lizzie a lesson so I thought I would write in my Journal while I had time for when we are together our tongues keep rattling so we have no time to think.

February 26, 1876

This is Ma's birthday and I should like to be at home but as my visit is not quite paid and the folks are insisting upon my staying a few days longer, I believe I shall stay till next Wednesday for I am having such a nice time. I got a letter from Lil and one from Ruf. I was real glad to hear from home. Ruf says he can't stand it, he is so awful lonesome and he wants me to come home as soon as I can. I suppose he forgets how lonesome I was when he was in Los Angeles He says they all had a splendid time at the masquerade. He knew hardly anybody till the masks were taken off. The dining rooms were crowded and everyone enjoyed the supper.

February 27, 1876

It commenced to rain in the night and has been showery all day. We were obliged to stay at home and read. I had a book called "Faithful & True." It was a library book belonging to Lizzie. The children had to stay in the house and hardly knew what to do with themselves. I hope it will not rain many days for the roads will get so rough for travel.

February 28, 1876

Very cloudy and the girl is afraid it will rain just as she gets the clothes hung out. I have been sewing all the morning and after lunch went down town to get my dress tried on. We will now eat supper and expect company in the evening.

February 29, 1876

The last day of February and I received two Valentines. I know Ruf sent them for they look like his work. Lizzie, the children and myself went to call on Mrs. Bailey and daughter, Mary. They are old friends of ours but we had not seen them for eight years. They have changed a good deal and thought we had also for now we are married and Lizzie has two children. They live at Hayes Valley and have a very pretty place. I must now get ready to go home tomorrow for I suppose Ruf and all the rest of the folks think I am staying a long time.

March 1, 1876

Got up early and was glad to find the weather clear if it was rather cold. Ate breakfast then started for the Valencia Street Depot. We arrived about twenty minutes before the train arrived. Lizzie was sorry to have me leave and stood on the platform as long as she could see the smoke. I had a seat on the outside of the stage and got home in time for hot soup. Everybody was glad to have me home again and I was glad to get back to them.

March 2, 1876

It begins to sprinkle and looks as if a storm was at hand. How lucky I was to get home before the rain. I found two letters waiting my return, one was from Clara telling what fine times she was having at surprise parties and candy pullings. The other was from Seneca Falls and contained news of my Aunt and cousins. Mary sent some handsome autumn leaves all sizes of Maple and they have been prepared with great care; she also sent her visiting card.

March 3, 1876

Have had so much to tell the folks about my visit that my tongue has not been quiet a moment since I got home. Even now I write a word and keep talking so as not to lose the time. Ma says I have given her a headache and Lil is getting the earache all on account of my tongue so I had better rest it.

March 4, 1876

Rain, rain, rain it pours and thunders like the mischief. Ruf says we will have a flood if it continues long. Today is Mrs. Lewis' birthday and I am to give her a silk neck-tie and Lil will give her two chromas of flowers. We are all getting ready for the new Masquerade Party which is to come off next Friday Eve. Wrote a letter and Postal Card order to San Francisco and will now read a story called "The Stewardess."

March 5, 1876

Very cloudy. Lil got ready for church this morning and just managed to get there before the rain. So it is now Lent. The Catholic bells are ringing and all the Irish in town are in church either morning or evening. Ma is reading "The Christian Keepsake" and Ruf is reading "The Vermont Journal." He was elected secretary of the "Grange" yesterday. I did not attend in the rain. Etta Tilton came to sing with us. Ruf went to church this evening, the sermon was from Luke on the prodigal son. Ruf says the congregation was disturbed by some rude men who were eating peanuts and candy. Phebe is six years old today. Mrs. Brown gave her a $2 gold piece and Ruf gave her a Mexican dollar made the year she was born. Ma gave her 2 1/2 gold piece so she is quite well off this birthday.

March 6, 1876

Rainy all day and the streets are muddy and wet. Wesley went on the noon stage, he will stay in the City two or three days. He has a number of orders for masks and other things to be worn at the Party. Ma received a letter from Alice Felt and I got a piece of music. Wrote two letters and sent sweet pea seeds in each. Went up to see Ellen and Mrs. Brown an hour, got an invitation to attend a surprise party at Mrs. Kelly's. She is preparing to move away and her friends wish to give her a party.

March 7, 1876

The weather is so stormy that I can find scarcely any thing to write about but rain. People are obliged to stay here over night for the roads are too bad to allow the stage to travel, so our house is quite full of delayed travelers. Little Everette was sick this morning with a high fever but is better now.

March 8, 1876

Wesley did not get home till this evening on account of rain, he bought a mask and false hair for me to wear to the Masquerade. I spent the afternoon with Fannie Frietas. Mrs. Brown and Milly are here to stay a few days with us. More rain. Moon changes tonight.

March 9, 1876

Weather clear. We have been very busy making a costume for Wesley. He is to be a negro dandy and I have made him a very funny coat with long tails and big buttons and a big junk necktie. Lil is to be a black nurse with baby. Mrs. Brown received her costume from the city today. She is to be Mother Goose and Mrs. Cook is to be a Chinaman.

March 10, 1876

I am so glad it does not rain for it would disappoint a great many if it did. Ma is making her suit. She is "Punch" and Mrs. Lewis is "Judy." They are so comic looking. I know everybody will laugh. I am to be "Minnehaha," and have a very fancy costume. Mr. McCurdy has loaned me his Indian bow, arrows and quiver and it helped to complete my rig. I have red striped stockings and fur shoes, a short dress and long black wig!

March 11, 1876

We had a capital time last night. So many were there and everyone seemed to enjoy themselves. Such a mass of funny objects you never saw. Everyone was laughing behind their masks and one could not tell who the other was. There were minstrels, negroes, Indians, Chinamen, Irish, a sheet and pillowcases, nurses and a Victoria Woodhull[5] who stood on a chair and rapped on her book for order and pretended to lecture. There were 80 people at supper but 120 at the party counting spectators. Mr. Hatch was Digger Indian and I did not know him at all. We promenaded together but did not recognize each other's walk.

March 12, 1876

It did seem as if I could not get sleep enough from being up late the night before, but I feel pretty bright today. Although, it is raining hard and looks very gloomy. Ellen, our chamber maid, left here this morning. She got mad because Father discharged the colored dish washer and she would not stay another day, so off she traveled, trunk and all. Mrs. Brown and Lil have gone to see little Everett, he is free from fever now but very weak. The birds are singing as loud as they can and I can hardly write. Received a letter from San Francisco and Ruf got one from Santa Monica.

---

[5] Victoria Woodhull, 1838-1927 was an American leader of the women's suffrage movement who ran for President of the United Staters in the 1872 election.

March 13, 1876

Pleasant weather. Ruf took Mrs. Brown out to ride. It was quite windy but they enjoyed the ride. Mrs. Fleming and Lizzie Wyman came to spend the afternoon, we found so much to talk about the party.

This is Jennie Dolloff's birthday; she is 18 years old. Ruf and I gave her an Album of Remembrance.

March 14, 1876

Nice weather, the roads are getting dry and people are getting encouraged, company on Monday brings company all the week. Mrs. Simmons and Alice Lea were here today. Ma and Mrs. Brown are visiting Ellen. Mrs. Metzger and her sister Eliza are there also. Mrs. Sexton, Mr. and Mrs. Levy, Mrs. Lewis and a few others are coming this evening to have some music and games.

March 15, 1876

Cloudy and looks some like rain. Mrs. Brown, Lil, Maria Levy, Millie and myself took a walk to the beach after breakfast. We had real fun going down, running, walking and resting, we spent from nine to eleven o'clock looking for pebbles and shells and chasing the waves. We then started for home; stopped on the way and went through the rooms of a new house, looked at the young trees planted in the garden and then came home very tired with our long walk. We brought several small curiously shaped shells and Mrs. Brown intends to take them to the City with her. Ma took the buggy and Fannie for a short drive this afternoon. Grace McGinty and Jennie Dolloff called on us. Mrs. Kelly moved to the City today.

March 16, 1876

Beautiful day! The road to Purissima is being ploughed and rolled and will be very smooth in a short time if it does not rain. Father went to San Francisco this morning, Mrs. Brown and I took a walk as far as the lumber yard and saw the machinery work. Mr. Simmons was busy making an ornamental door. Milly and Amy Sexton joined us there and went with us to the flour Mill. It was not running at the time but we had a good chance to see all parts of the building and the large metal water wheel outside and the running creek. We sat down on the grass beyond the mill in a very romantic spot near what is called "The Grove." On our way home we stopped to admire a fine garden and leaned over the fence as we did so, but in turning to leave the place we found our hands, shawls and dresses full of fresh white paint. What a scene! We hastened home to get our clothes cleaned and managed to get most of it off. A young lady gave me a piece of chewing gum and I find it very hard to keep my mouth still.

Dr. McCurdy and Miss Morey are playing the Piano belonging to Mr. Maguire the Band Master.

March 17, 1876

St. Patrick's Day dawned very foggy. The fog whistle is blowing and we can scarcely see across the street. There is to be a ball tonight and I suppose it will be well attended as St. Patrick's balls generally are. Wrote a letter, received a "Musical Review." We are invited out to dinner today but will not go. I am going to the Public School in the afternoon to hear the speaking.

Father came home on the noon stage. The brass band have been playing a number of tunes in front of the Hotel in honor of the day.

March 18, 1876

The anniversary of our wedding day arrived. It does not seem possible that a year has passed which is a good sign that it has been a happy one. Ruf took me out to ride and we went as far as we could without getting in the mud. I gave him a Russian leather cigar case and he was delighted with it. He had not been to the city and had no chance to buy anything for me so he gave me a silver dollar with the year 1876 which will keep me in remembrance of the time. Ma, Lil, Mrs. Brown and Milly went to spend the day with Mrs. Metzgar and did not get home till nine o'clock. Mrs. Lewis and Mrs. Boyd spent the evening with me while Ruf went to the Lodge.

March 19, 1876

A beautiful day makes its' appearance. Lil went to church this morning but got there too late to hear the text. She says there was quite a congregation. Alice came home today; she intends to teach school tomorrow and has a horse and saddle so that she can ride. Ruf went to Church this evening with Mr. Peugh.

March 20, 1876

We have very fine weather, so warm and pleasant. Mrs. Boyd came in to show us some mosses she had been floating. Mrs. Brown and Milly went home to the City today and we miss them very much. Ellen is here. Ma took her out for a ride as far as Amesport Landing. Mary Davids has been here all the afternoon. Lizzie Pitcher, Mrs. Rosenblum, Laura and Mrs. Metzgar were here this evening. I have been reading "Days of Seventy-Six," a very fine story of the war. Lil and I went to see Mrs. Nichols and the girls today. Ruf says he set up six buggies in a few hours. I thought he was very smart, but when he took me to the shop to see them I found six Irish buggies or wheelbarrows standing up by the fence.

March 21, 1876

The wind blows very hard, it shakes the house like old fun. People are having trees put out in front of their houses and it will be very pretty when they begin to grow. They have lattice frames to prevent cattle destroying them. Received a letter from Lizzie. Learned a new instrumental piece, "Persian Rose March."

March 22, 1876

Still windy and very unpleasant. Father went to Redwood today. He was summoned on the jury. He drove over with the buggy and two horses, Tib and George. Mr. Wyman accompanied him. He says it blew so hard they came near losing their hats a dozen times. Ruf and I will spend the evening with Ellen as she is generally lonely for Wesley does not get home till after ten o'clock. Fannie Freitas has just gone home. She has been here quite a while. We loaned her some books to read.

March 23, 1876

Calm today and very pleasant. Amy Sexton is six years old and she received a great many presents. I collected a large bundle of clothing for my wash woman. She will think it quite a gift. A lady came on the stage who is canvassing for "Hills Manual." She got several subscribers today.

March 24, 1876

The weather is very fine. Ellen and Mrs. Rosenblum have gone to visit Mrs. Guerrero who lives quite a distance from here and they will not return till dark. Ma and I called to see Miss Hunter a lady who is 60 years old. She is as spry as a girl and has always been in good health till a few days ago while giving a music lesson she fainted and has been failing ever since. She is now out of her mind at times but we hope she will recover. Lil has a headache and is lying down.

March 25, 1876

This is Wesley's birthday and I gave him a box of handkerchiefs and some shaving soap which was the best I could get out here, but not much of a gift. We all had a look at the eclipse of the sun through a piece of smoked glass. It was a pretty sight at first, but a small portion was eclipsed but finally it reached almost half and lasted about two hours.

Lil and myself were out taking a walk and met Etta Tilton and Jennie Dolloff. They are on the committee for the Leap Year Ball that is to come off on the 31st and they want us to join them so as to make a larger party but we declined.

March 26, 1876

Weather clear and delightful. The churches were full today. The Protestant Church had a large congregation for the roads are in better condition for traveling and a great many live out of town. The Catholic Church was full on account of one of their Holy Days and they are in some way obliged to be there or displease the priest. Phebe has a terrible toothache and Dr. McCurdy has extracted it. He was obliged to give her a dose of chloroform before he could get her to be quiet enough to allow him to examine the tooth. It had a very long prong and he was afraid of breaking the jaw.

Went to church this evening and heard a lecture on "Unbelieving." It was splendid and I hope will do some good. There were but few present, but we enjoyed the lecture for Mr. Hazzard, the pastor had written a kind note to several young men who are in the habit of disturbing the congregation. They got offended and would not attend church which was much better than going for sport and to ridicule the pastor.

March 27, 1876

Pleasant again today. Received a letter from Santa Barbara and a yard of lace enclosed. Fannie Freitas has been here all afternoon. Mrs. Nichols and Mrs. Lewis came in this evening.

March 28, 1876

Quite windy and beginning to be dusty. Received a letter from Clara in which she writes that we may expect to see her soon. She is coming over to spend a few weeks with us and we will be very glad to have her with us.

Mrs. Gordon of Redwood is here. She intends to

stay a few days at the Hotel and then go to the ranch for a week at San Gregorio. She played a game of "Snap" with us and I do not know when I enjoyed a hearty laugh so well for she did not understand the game and would grab all the cards whether they belonged to her or not. It was so funny to see how excited she got but we thought it rather cool to lose our cards. Ma, Lil and I took a nice walk along the edge of the creek and by the jail. We then stopped a few moments to see Mrs. Pitcher.

March 29, 1876

The wind is blowing very hard and we can scarcely walk. Mrs. Rosenblum came in awhile this morning. I got a letter from Lizzie. Went out and stayed all the afternoon but ought to have been home ironing instead. Houses around here are getting painted, most of them white.

March 30, 1876

Still windy and unpleasant. Wrote two letters this morning, then took a short walk, bought some new muslin of Mr. Rosenblum. Mr. and Mrs. Chapin and two children came on the stage today. They live in the redwoods and had been to the City on a visit.

Ruf came home tonight with a large paper bag full of peanuts, they were fresh and crispy, being roasted just to my taste. He has been to the Free Mason's Lodge every evening this week as they have some important business and were obliged to call a meeting. The lodge room is directly opposite the Hotel and I can see the light through the curtains.

March 31, 1876

The last day of the month is blowing itself along. People can scarcely keep on their feet in the streets. This evening the young ladies of this town are to give a Leap Year Ball and they anticipate a fine time. The girls are to foot the bills themselves and one or two are obliged to hire buggies to go after the young men they have invited as they live some distance from town. Ruf says he feels a little slighted because the girls did not give him an invitation. I tell him they would be foolish to ask a married man.

April 1, 1876

April Fools' Day and its many jokes come to cheer us a little. Ruf made a fool of me first thing after breakfast. He sent me to the window to see a beautiful sight and before I stopped to think he began to laugh. Almost everybody in the house got caught before night. I went to the shop and told Ruf that a gentleman wished to see him at the Hotel. "Well," he said. "Ask him to call at the shop. Tell him this is my place for transacting business." So I did not make much out of him but got fooled myself instead. Many are tired on account of being up late last night to the Ball and do not feel lively enough to try their tricks today.

April 2, 1876

A nice sun shine greets our eyes. The Church bells are ringing and I just prepare myself to go. I will finish this, this evening. Went to Church and heard the continuation of the lecture of last Sabbath, this eve was about Laws of God and Laws of Nature. There was quite a large number present, a collection was taken up in aid of the Sunday School.

April 3, 1876

All of yesterday's sun is swallowed up in the fog of today, we can scarcely see across the street. Fannie Freitas and her husband just went to the City. They took a buggy as far as San Mateo, then the cars to S.F. and returned in the evening. They say it rained hard all day.

April 4, 1876

Pleasant today. A large party of gentlemen and ladies went down to the beach to a clam bake. They had a splendid time. While the men dug clams and caught fish, the girls fixed a place to cook and when the time came, made clam chowder, fried the fish, baked potatoes and soon had a dinner fit for a king. They each took a plate, sat on the sand and enjoyed the feast. One of the gentlemen made the coffee and it was delicious.

April 5, 1876

Another nice day. Several of the girls hired horses and took a ride on horseback. Lil and Ma went for a buggy ride while I spent the afternoon with Ellen.

Amelia brought her baby out for the first time and it is a real nice little fellow. Received a letter from Cousin Robert called The Centennial, it is written on printing paper and is very large. It contains more news than twenty common letters and is an odd looking affair. I shall have a good deal of fun trying to answer it according to his. I intend to buy legal paper and keep pasting it together till I have it four yards in length. Then I will collect all the nonsense I can think of to fill it. Robert says, "In all nonsense there is some sense," but I guess he will have to scratch for the sense in mine. I mean to write a regular burlesque on his, he pretends to be so very patriotic and full of the idea of celebrating this grand centennial that I shall endeavor to tease him.

April 6, 1876

Father and Ruf went to San Francisco. They started at six o'clock and will take the cars at San Mateo station, they will come home tomorrow. Both intend going to the Odd Fellow's Lodge this evening and I believe Ruf will join the Encampment. If he does we may go East in September when the Brigade goes to Philadelphia. Father belongs to the Brigade and will parade with them.

April 7, 1876

Nice weather. Received a letter from Los Angeles, one from Santa Barbara and one from San Francisco. Wrote one to "New Age."

Bought a rubber stamp with my name, box of cards, brush ink, pads and everything for making cards, clothing etc. The agent is here, Ma and Lil also got a stamp of their names. Mr. Levy is moving into his house today. The furniture came in the morning. Lil is working in the garden. Ma is reading "The Call" and I am writing in my Journal, so you can see we are busy. Now how I want to know what you are doing. I can almost guess you are in Oakland visiting Susie and helping Mr. Smith get ready to go East or else you are at home teaching some little urchins their ABC, how I envy you.

April 8, 1876

Just as I came down to write a few letters Fannie Freitas came in, so we had a pleasant time for we went into one of the pleasant sunny rooms while Ma practiced the Piano and we chatted away and did some sewing also.

Received a letter from Dubuque, one from Ottawa and another from San Mateo so I shall have my hands full of writing for awhile.

April 9, 1876

Weather pleasant. As I did not go to church, Mrs. Hartley and I took turns in reading a French book. We made many mistakes for we had forgotten a great many words and the French verbs are so hard to remember that we were obliged to puzzle our brains a little.

It is Palm Sunday, the Catholic Church is crowded. Buggies and wagons are standing in line around the Church and as the members come out, each has a piece of tree in hand which has been blest by Father Velentini

We all went to evening services. The chapter was St. John two through twenty second verse. Although his discourse was very interesting, I noticed several men asleep. You will think perhaps that if I had been looking at the Pastor I would not have seen others. Well no, I could scarcely be blamed for doing so as the men were directly in front of my pew and as one fell in a doze he threw his head back, another sent his noodle forward and made quite a ludicrous scene. Once in a while the pastor would speak rather loud, then both would start and wake up for a time.

April 10, 1876

Nice day. Ma and Lil took a short ride. I received a letter from Mrs. Price in Panamint. They intended to start from there some time ago but were delayed and will leave tomorrow the 11th April. She says they had a feast of ice cream last week and I could almost taste it when her letter got here. I went to see Mrs. Davids this morning and she showed me some very fine plants she has growing in a sunny window. Mary is getting ready for a trip to Pescadero.

April 11, 1876

Ruf and I left town right after breakfast and had a delightful ride up to the Mill. The roads were good excepting a few places that men are now working on.

Found everything in order at the house. Ruf was busy all afternoon digging around plants and currant bushes. The climate is much warmer up here as the place is surrounded by mountains.

April 12, 1876

As we remained here overnight we are now preparing to go back to town. I have been oiling the sewing machine, airing the trunks and letting sun in the rooms. After a drive of two hours we again find ourselves at the hotel. I feel pretty tired after the ride but soon forgot my fatigue in the pleasure of seeing Clara whom I have been expecting so long. She came on the stage today. I suppose you have met her, she is quite a pleasant girl, has considerable good sense and is a very dear friend of mine. Well she is here safe and sound though terribly shaken up I fear and will require a good rest.

April 13, 1876

Got up bright this morning for the sun was shining in the window and would not permit me to enjoy sleep longer. Clara, Lil and I have been sewing, reading and talking together all the afternoon. Toward evening we began to think of games and played a great many funny ones.

Clara taught us one called "Buzz." It is played by counting and when you get to seven or a multiple of seven, you say "Buzz." It made us laugh for we would often forget and say the number, to make it more amusing when five is reached say "Buzz" and then "Buzz" at seven.

April 14, 1876

Weather foggy in the morning but sunshine in the afternoon. This is Good Friday and almost every Catholic goes to Church. Many Protestants go also to see how the services are conducted.

Clara and Lil were invited to the School to hear the children speak. They went about two o'clock and spent an hour pleasantly. They say some of the older pupils did very well and had quite long pieces to recite. After school was dismissed, Mrs. Hartley took them through the building.

April 15, 1876

Saturday clear and busy. Beauty is singing as loud as he can in the sitting room window; Fannie Stegman was here quite a while this afternoon as she is teaching all the rest of the week, she has to do her visiting on Saturday. She called on Mrs. Levy also. Clara gave me a nice song, "Pass Under the Rod" and I have been practicing it.

April 16, 1876

Easter Sunday and everybody who is able is at

church. We had a sermon suitable for the day so Clara says as she and Lil were there.

Ruf and I went this evening, the text was Acts 2nd chapter 6th verse and finished in a kind of lecture inspiration of the spirit of God.

April 17, 1876

Quite a cloudy day, looks like rain. A German lady with her baby came to see us, we were amused because I offered her a fig and she thought it was a peach. Clara has been writing a letter to her father and composing a piece of "poetry" for Phebe to speak next Friday. Alice Felt was here. She spent the day and night at San Gregorio and rode to school from there. Ruf is getting ready to take Clara out for a ride. Wrote two letters and must now write one to Lottie Searles. Clara has been teaching me to make hair pin crochet. Mrs. Sexton spent the evening with us and we had a game of "Authors," we always have fun when we teach a new hand to play.

April 18, 1876

The morning was beautiful so Clara and I took a nice little walk down the street. After dinner Ruf started for Pescadero to be present at the Free Mason's Lodge tonight. Mr. Davids and Mr. Freitas went also. Lil went to spend the afternoon with Ellen Johnston so Clara and I went to see Fannie F and Cora Levey. Dr. McCurdy came in about five o'clock and we all ate supper together after which we had music and singing till almost ten o'clock.

April 19, 1876

Clara slept with me last night and Ma awoke us early this morning, in fact before the gong had sounded for breakfast, so we jumped up lively as it was so pleasant and warm.

Ma, Mrs. Lewis and Lil went to the moss beach and as it is quite a distance and took them quite a while to go, Clara and I went to spend the afternoon with my sister-in-law. We took our crocheting to pretend we were industrious. Just as I write Ellen sends word for us to delay our visit as she has an invitation to go to the beach also and as I was writing beforehand we were cheated out of our visit so in the afternoon Clara and I rigged ourselves up and went out to make calls. We were fortunate in finding the ladies at home. We first called on Mrs. Nichols, found two other ladies there and enjoyed a quiet chat for an hour. We then went to see Lizzie Pitcher and she made us feel at home at once. She entertained us by explaining photographs to us and talking of new books. We next called on Jennie Dolloff and Etta Tilton and after spending a time pleasantly there, walked home declaring we had spent a "very pleasant afternoon."

We found the beach party back and as they had started early they ate their lunch on the beach. They say when they go there the coffee was hot.

April 20, 1876

Awake early, ate breakfast, came upstairs to clean the room up a little, finished my piece of hairpin crochet, gave Beauty a bath, went to the store, bought some pink ribbon, 2 yards of Nero white ribbon, 2 yards of embroidery, a back comb for Ma and a paper of pins. Clara bought two yards of blue ribbon. We met a man with a basket of oranges and bought some, also some candy then came home to dinner. Father and Dr. McCurdy went to Pescadero. Ellen Johnson, Lizzie Pinkham and her baby came to stay all afternoon. Etta Tilton came as soon as school was out for she was formerly a school mate of Mrs. Pinkham. Mrs. Ganline came with her baby to stay a little while and altogether we enjoyed our company very much. In the evening Mrs. Hartley came in but was called for in an hour by Miss Morey who wished to see her on business. Alice Felt intended to come also but was kept at home to do some sewing she promised to finish this week.

Clara, Ma, Ruf, Lil and I had a fine time guessing Proverbs. We had some fun too getting the large words in as a disguise.

April 21, 1876

Very windy and rain this morning and about noon it began to rain and continued all the afternoon, the wind blew and it was very gloomy but I suppose it was a great benefit to the farmers, also to the roads.

Ruf bought a box of strawberries for me and I relish them very much, mostly because they are so dear I suppose. We played a game of name guessing, we took a letter and would think of all the girls names commencing with that letter. It was a pleasant past time for evening. Ruf came upstairs about 8 1/2 o'clock and Ma read a story "Yankee and Dutchman." I also read the "Circuit Preacher" aloud.

April 22, 1876

The weather today was right opposite what it was yesterday. The sun is bright and Wesley is planting trees in the garden. It is now about 5 o'clock P.M. Ma and Clara have been riding, they were gone two hours and rode along the beach beyond Amesport Landing. Clara was delighted with the ocean view and now feeling a little tired. She is sitting by the window floating some sea moss. Lil went out to call on Etta Tilton and has just returned.

April 23, 1876
The Sabbath

How still the morning of the hallowed day!
Mute is the voice of rural labour, hushed
The plough boy's whistle, the milkmaid's song,
The scythe lies glittering in the dewy wreath
of tedded grass, mingled with fading flowers,
Moth, dove-like wings, peace o'er you village,
The dizzying mill wheel rests: the anvil's din
Hath ceased; all, all around is quietness.
Less fearful on this day, the limping hare
Stops, and looks back, and stops, and looks on man,
her deadliest foe. The toil-worn horse, set free,

Unheedful of the pasture, roams at large;
And, as his stiff unwieldy, bulk he rolls,
His iron armed hoofs gleam in the morning ray.
But chiefly man the day of rest enjoys,
Hail Sabbath! Thee I hail, the poor man's day.

April 24, 1876

A pleasant day. Clara went home today and Lill went with her. She will stay in Redwood till Wednesday when she will go to the Odd Fellow's picnic then return home the day after. We miss them very much and I felt very lonely all the afternoon although Fannie and Cora came in for a while. They could not fill the place of Clara and when I look at the arm chair I could cry. Mrs. Lewis came in the evening to see us.

April 25, 1876

Got up before the gong rang this morning but did not get breakfast till Father and Ma came down. Ruf was in a hurry to go to the shop so he ate and I sat at the table merely for company.

Went to the store to buy some things for Mrs. Johnson at the mill. Got a straw hat for Della and some gingham to make shirts for the boys.

Mr. Hazard and Dr. McCurdy came in the parlor a while this afternoon and talked about the affairs of the church. They are having the children prepare for a S.S. concert to be given next Sunday evening. Ma has been floating mosses all morning and gave the minister some.

April 26, 1876
Redwood City visit

The weather has been beautiful all day, rather warm about noon but nice weather for the Odd Fellows picnic. Father and Ma drove over in the buggy with Fannie. Ruf went in his buggy and did not get home till late. They say there were 20,000 people on the grounds and all enjoying themselves in a grand style. Ruf saw many from the City that he knew. He ate lunch with Clara and Lil by invitation. He says there were sack races, fat women's race, young girls' races, hurdle races for men and boys race, horseback riding, dancing and everything that could possibly be there to increase the pleasure of the crowd. I wanted to go very much but the ride was too long. So, I stayed at home reading, sewing and writing to my heart's content.

April 27, 1876

Father and Ma came home about eleven o'clock this morning, Lil came on the stage. They were in San Mateo all night as they went to the circus and it was too late to drive home. They liked the horse parade very much but what interested them most was a sight of the woman weighing seven hundred pounds. Her waist was one yard and three quarters around and they saw a very small woman thirty eight years.

April 28, 1876

It was so pleasant today. Mrs. Metzgar thought she would bring the baby and spend the day with us. So we enjoyed her visit very much. Her baby is five months old and so cunning, she puts a pillow on the floor and he will lie on it for hours and kick and laugh to himself.

Lil brought a nice large orange to me from the picnic. Mr. Shelly bought some and Clara sent one to me. Ruf took me out to ride a little way this morning but I soon became tired. There was speaking at the school 3 o'clock and Phoebe did very well in speaking the piece Clara composed for her. Amy spoke "The Busy Bee."

April 29, 1876

Ruf went up to the mill as soon as breakfast was over. I went to the stable and sat on some hay, watching him harness the horses and saw him start off. He did not intend to come back tonight, but a gentleman came over to buy one of Ruf's horses named Flash, and be rode up to the Mill to see Ruf, so they came down together to make their bargain.

Ruf has gone to the Lodge now so I have a good chance to write my journal and to have a good chew on my gum.

April 30, 1876

The last day of April is made of sunshine and

shadow. We had quite a shower last night. Lil went to church this morning and in the evening. Father Ma, Lil, Ruf and I went to the S.S. concert at the church. The exercises were not as good as usual but it was owing to several of the best singers being absent. However the children who spoke pieces did very well indeed. They took up a collection of $7.35 cts for new papers for the school.

May 1, 1876

May Day has been quite pleasant excepting. Late in the afternoon the wind blew very hard. The day schools had a picnic in "Hatch's Grove." Lil went and she says the children seem to have a good time swinging, jumping and enjoying themselves. There was also a Granger picnic at Pescadero and a great many went from here to the picnic.

Ruf went up to the Mill today and intends to stay a few days. Father and Ma took a ride and I spent the afternoon with the watchmaker's wife. She was quite pleased to see me and almost the first thing she did was to open the baby's mouth and say, "See, he got nudder toot."

May 2, 1876

Got up rather late this morning because I had slept alone and had the curtains all down so it would look dark. I found the family had all got ahead of me, and Lil was weeding in the garden.

Received a letter from Sherman & Hyde, one from Cousin Mary and one from Ruf's sister in Byron. Minn. so I shall have quite a writing time. Cora Leavy and

Fannie Freitas came and remained to tea with us, and in the evening Mrs. Lewis and a Ella Olive from Stockton came so we had a pleasant time singing, playing, and a game of "Snap." They all went home at ten o'clock accompanied by Dr. McCurdy.

May 3, 1876

The wind is blowing very hard and the dust flies. Mrs. Davids came in a while this morning to see Ma. Miss Stegman came this afternoon to see me. Mr. and Mrs. Ames left for the East. I got weighed 132 1/2 lbs. Lil 118 1/2. Called to see Etta Tilton. Beauty is singing as loud as he can and keeps up his everlasting trill that Clara likes to hear so well. Redwood has it's fair tonight. I see by the paper that "Blind Tom" is to play piano for the fair. I should like to hear him. If the folks have gone to a donation party for our minister, I will tell of it.

May 4, 1876

Fine day but windy. The party for the Moss Beach started at 10 o'clock this morning. Ma, Lil and Amy went in the buggy. Mr. & Mrs. Lewis, Mrs. Sexton, Mrs. Davids and Ella Olive went in a spring wagon.[6] They took a big lunch and as it happened one did not

---

[6] Spring Wagon: A four wheel vehicle drawn by horses having a square box and between two and four movable seat boards. It was a general purpose wagon, used for transportation of either goods or passengers.

know what the other intended to take. The consequence was each party took a dozen boiled eggs so they had a regular egg lunch. Ma took a can of coffee so did Mrs. Lewis and they say when they got to the beach the coffee was hot. No wonder. Ma had her can boiling hot and a grain sack rolled around it. Then it formed a comfortable seat for Amy and could not help keeping hot. The wind blew so hard they were not able to get any moss and were quite disappointed. Lil has just been telling me about the donation party last eve. She says a great many were there who brought provisions and they also collected $50 in money which was good for this place. Mom sent $5.00 and two nice grape pies. They had a long table set and plenty on it to eat. After supper which was ten o'clock they went to Good Templar's Hall to play games.

May 5, 1876

Still windy the house was full today on account of good traveling a great many are visiting Pescadero. Mr. Taft has put the evening stage on and it makes business brisk. I made an apron today and two yards of hair pin crochet with a spool of linen thread. It is so pretty and strong too. Ruf just come home he has been away since Monday the 1st. He is preparing to go to the Lodge this evening. Mrs. Lewis invited us to come and see her so we are going till after Lodge closes when the gentlemen will call for us.

May 6, 1876

Very warm and pleasant today, no wind. Ella
Tilton came from San Mateo to visit her sister and she
and Etta came to see us this afternoon and took tea
with us. We enjoyed it very much. Mrs. Hartley came
in a while in the evening. I forgot to say Ruf took me
for a short drive early this morning.

May 7, 1876

Another nice day. Lil and Alice went to church in
the morning. Mrs. Hartley and sister from San
Francisco took a buggy ride to the Mill. The presiding
Elder will preach this evening. We will go to hear him.

May 8, 1876

Very warm today. It is what we call earthquake
weather. I must tell you of last night's sermon
preached by Mr. Wythe, the Elder, a very smart man,
His discourse was from the death of Christ or rather
the crucifixion. He says Christ was not put to death
by the Jews, as many believe, but that being nailed to
the cross and knowing he had to starve to death, he
naturally died of a broken heart.

He spoke very affecting concerning the subject
and was listened to with much attention. Mary
Davids, Belle Nichols and Jennie Dolloff were here
quite a while this afternoon and as it is Monday, we
shall look for company the rest of the week.

May 9, 1876

I will begin by saying our expected visitors came today. Also Mrs. Lee spent the afternoon. She brought a magnificent bouquet for me. Roses, lily, daisies, pansies, geranium, laurel, honeysuckle and snapdragon, enough to make three good size vases full. Fanny Freitas also came about two o'clock and went home at five. Ruf is at the mill and I miss him a good deal. The weather has been warm today. Rec one letter.

May 10, 1876

Weather gloomy and very foggy all day. Could not raise enough sun to bleach a single spray of sea moss which I had in my window and was obliged to keep fire in my room. Ma and Mrs. Sexton went to San Francisco this morning. They left here about six o'clock with Fanny in the buggy. I suppose they had a very unpleasant ride for it was almost a rain. Our company for today was Mrs. Allsop, a lady from San Jose who took dinner with us and then staid part of the afternoon and at three o'clock Ella Olive the young lady from Sacramento came. She staid to dinner and we had some nice games in the evening. Mrs. Lewis also came after dark and we had singing till ten. Miss Ella has a sweet voice and sang "Father Will Settle the Bill" very nicely. I do really believe we are doomed to have company the whole week.

May 11, 1876

Weather still dismal. Wrote to Cousin Mary. Bought a box of fresh strawberries and they were delicious. Three wagon loads of folks left here early this morning to go fishing in Purissima Creek. Half of them were ladies. They took a lunch with them. Mrs. Davids and Ellen came to see us in the afternoon. So far the saying comes true.

May 12, 1876

Rather cloudy today. Mr. and Mrs. Lewis, Ella and Lil went on a fishing excursion beyond the Mill. I sent a package of papers to Ruf. They got home near evening after having a splendid time. They caught three fish. Ruf drove down this afternoon and stayed a couple of hours. Then went back. He says the folks have moved out of our house and he is afraid to leave it alone for any length of time. Mrs. Dolloff came and sat with me three hours in the afternoon and Mrs. Nichols came in the evening. Ma got home from the city just at dusk very tired. She brought a very handsome present for Rosanna a cloak and hat. Also some things for Lil.

May 13, 1876

A nice day. I began to write letters this morning and kept it up till almost dinner time. I had three business letters to answer for Ruf. Etta Tilton came to stay a while today and I enjoyed her visit very much. She expects to have vacation in a few weeks. Ella Olive went home today. Mrs. Lewis spent the evening here. Ruf came down and will stay till Monday. He was too tired to attend the Lodge.

May 14, 1876

The sun has been shining brightly all day. Lil went to church. Mr. Curry preached, and seemed glad to see his congregation again. He has been away seven months and has a church at Woodland. Ruf is now lying of the sofa reading his Vermont Journal. Ma bought a book for me called "Sevenoaks" by J. G. Holland. A baby was christened at the Catholic Church.

May 15, 1876

Very gloomy. There was such a heavy fog and mist this morning that it was equal to a rain. No need of sprinkling the flowers this weather. Father has just set out some more gum trees. A dear little canary flew into my window early this morning. It seemed delighted when it saw Beauty's cage and tried to get in. So I opened the door and it went in and jumped into the swing, seeming perfectly at home. It took a bath and ate seed from the fountain so it is a tame bird that has escaped from its' cage. I was afraid Beauty would pick at it but I see that it soon began to consider the house its' own and picked at Beauty. Mrs. Alsop and Mrs. Nichols were here today.

May 16, 1976

Very foggy. I caught a dreadful cold sleeping in the draught. Wrote a letter to Lizzie and sent her a piece of vocal music. The wind blows so hard we cannot go outside the door unless we get raised off our feet. I mended Ruf's pants this morning and had plenty of work on them. The whole sit down was split so that I was obliged to put a large piece in them. They are too tight for him. Belle and Carrie were here after school. Lil gave Belle two pretty aprons that were too short for herself. There I go coughing, sneezing, and blowing like sixty. It is delightful to have a cold.

May 17, 1876

Pleasant weather. I went to see Mrs. Lewis and sat with her helping her to sew a long time. Mrs. Lewis gave me a dish of cherries. I had all the strawberries I could eat for breakfast, dinner and supper. They were brought to the door in a wagon.

May 18, 1876

Warm and pleasant. Ma went to Moss Beach at 11 to 6. Got some nice sprays. I have done but little sewing, reading or anything else today but sleep. I felt so sleepy I laid down on the sofa and was sound in a few minutes. My cold is not much better.

May 19, 1876

The ladies of the Catholic Church gave a Festival in Pacific Hall last evening to raise money for the Priest. It seems Father Velentini borrowed $500 dollars from the Bishop of San Francisco with which to purchase a fine three hundred and fifty dollar buggy. Fast horse, elegant buggy robes etc. using the whole amount of the borrowed money for the articles. He also promised to return the five hundred dollars at the end of a year expecting to get it from his church people, but failing to get it the Bishop seized the horse and buggy and has offered it for sale. So the Catholic friends joined together to get enough money to buy his lordship another outfit. They had ice cream and strawberries and danced till morning. I have not yet heard of how much money they made.

Ruf came home this afternoon and will go back to the mill in the morning.

May 20, 1876

Nice weather. I have been mending old cloth all the morning and my fingers are as rough as graders. Received two letters from S.F. Ella Tilton, Jennie Dolloff, Fannie Freitas and Mary Davids were here in the afternoon and we had so much fun. I laughed till I felt bruised all over. Lil went to visit Cora Levey.

May 21, 1876

A gentleman and his daughter arrived last night from the City. He wants to let her board here for a week. They came in the parlor about 9 o'clock and I was sitting on the sofa with my shoes off getting ready to go to bed. So I only bowed when introduced and got along very well till coaxed to play piano. Then I was in a pickle. I begged to be excused but the gentleman insisted upon just one tune. Of course it would have been as easy to play a dozen as one if I could have got up so I have a terrible time of it till Ma began to show her (?) then the old Gent let me alone. I don't want to be caught in that fix again. Lil went to church this morning. I wanted to go real bad for it was a beautiful day. Ruf drove down to see me in the afternoon and scolded me for catching such a heavy cold. I have a ringworm on my finger and must put some black ink on it to kill it. I have a large dish of fresh strawberries on the table beside me. Also a bowl of slippery elm[7] which is very inviting. Did you know it is excellent for a cold? It is!

May 22, 1876

Pleasant weather. Spent the morning in walking, in fact did too much of it for I was so tired in the evening that I went to bed about suppertime and Ma brought a plate of toast and preserve quinces for me

---

[7] Slippery elm (Ulmus rubra) is a species of elm native to eastern North America. The inner bark has long been used as a demulcent and is still produced commercially for this purpose.

to eat. Miss Alice Wolfe (the young lady who is boarding here from the City) Lil and myself have been preparing rhubarb for pie fruit. Ma bought a large quantity of it and we were almost all the afternoon peeling it. When we had finished Ma treated us to a bag of cherries which we ate with a relish.

May 23, 1876

Very rainy, cold, windy and unpleasant today. We had a shower in the morning which sprinkled the streets nicely. Miss Alice has been in my room most of the day. I like her very much. She is easy to become acquainted with and is very interesting. She told us of Sacramento where she has been engaged in teaching three years. We then read together, crocheted, played piano and passed our time pleasantly. Ma bought a game of "Star Authors" and we like it so much. Got a letter from San Francisco from a man who wanted to buy one of Ruf's horses so I sent it up to the Mill.

May 24, 1876

This has been a beautiful day. Miss Wolfe and I took a buggy ride in the morning. We went as far as Amesport Landing then on the county road to the toll gate. I have not been to ride for sometime and enjoyed it very much. Jennie Dolloff was here this afternoon. Mary Davids came and spent the evening. She brought a very handsome crocheted bib for Rosanna. Mary made it herself. She got the pattern at Pescadero.

May 25, 1876

Nice weather. Went out visiting this afternoon and was sent for as Mr. Price's wife and two children came over from San Mateo to see me. They have been but a few weeks from Peniment and intend to start for the Centennial next Thursday. They will remain here overnight and go back to San Mateo tomorrow.

May 26, 1876

Another pleasant day. Ellen Johnston came at one o'clock and stayed till five. We had a nice long chat together. I am to make a quilt, or at least cut the blocks and each of the girls are to make one block and stamp their names in the center white patch. There is a Ball tonight and the folks are dancing as hard as can be. Mrs. Lewis got home today.

May 27, 1876

Warm and delightful. Received a letter of eight pages from Clara, one almost as long from Martha and a letter from Lizzie containing some pretty crochet trimming for pillow slips. Joe McGinty is very sick with brain fever.[8] I've had lots of company today. Mrs. Hartley, Etta Tilton, Jennie Dolloff, Emina Dawson, Alice Wolfe and Fannie Freitas. I had quite a room full

---

[8]Brain fever: a medical condition where a part of the brain becomes inflamed and causes symptoms that present as fever.

for a while. Fannie staid till ten o'clock when her husband came from the Lodge.

May 28, 1876

Ruf came down this morning. He left the Mill at four o'clock and got here at six. I was sound asleep when he knocked at the door. Lil and Miss Wolfe went to morning service. I went last Sunday evening but got so tired I found it difficult to sit still so I guess I will not go again till I feel stronger. The sun shines brightly today. Beauty sings and everything seems happy. A lady sent me a very large and beautiful bouquet from her garden.

May 29, 1876

Joe McGinty died this morning and Ruf was with the family till two o'clock in the afternoon. Miss Wolfe, Lil and I went to the store this evening and got weighed. I weigh 138 lbs. Lil 118 1/2. Miss Wolf 136.

May 30, 1876

Very windy all day. Received a letter from Mrs. Kelly, wrote one to Clara. Mrs. Davids spent the afternoon with me. I have been sewing my patch quilt it is pink and white. Mrs. Lewis has been tucking a linen skirt for me and it is very pretty.

May 31, 1876

Not quite as windy as yesterday. This is Father's birthday. Ma gave him a gold charm for his watch chain. It holds her picture inside and on the outside is a tent to represent the Grand Encampment and the three links with F. L. T. one letter in each link. On the back is engraved (Jos Schuyler G.G. No 1 1876.) He is delighted with it. Lil gave him a new pair of gloves and the game of "Lotto." Ruf gave him a choice cigar and I gave a silver napkin ring with his name on it. Joe McGinty was buried at eleven o'clock this morning. His father being a Catholic, had him laid in the Mission ground. He was just 18 years of age and very much liked by all who knew him. The school was closed so that all had an opportunity to attend the funeral. There were eighty three buggies, twenty on horseback and the Good Templars (of which he was a member) walked behind the rest.

June 1, 1876

A terrible foggy day. The fog whistle is blowing and makes a very dismal sound. There is but little of interest today so I find nothing to write. Ma is floating mosses, Lil is trimming a night dress, Miss Wolfe is making some hairpin crochet for an apron and now I am going to mend my stockings.

June 2, 1876

Sun shining all day, quite the contrary of yesterday. Wrote a letter to Martha and did my ironing. Mary Davids, Miss Wolfe, Mrs. Sexton and myself had several games of "Authors" and "Snap" in the afternoon. I went around toward evening to give Etta Tilton, Jennie Dolloff and Alice Felt the patches for the blocks they are to make for my quilt. There was speaking at the school at three o'clock as this is the last day of school for three weeks. Father and Ma went down to the beach to see the men catch fish. Ruf came down to the Lodge.

June 3, 1876

Went up to see Ellen in the morning and stayed till noon. Miss Wolfe met her mother, two sisters, and four brothers at the stage. They will keep house around the corner from here and make quite a pack of wolves. Mrs. Hartley gave me a very pretty dress for a baby and a bib.

June 13, 1876

Here you will perceive I have made a skip of nine or ten days. Well it has been quite an important skip too as it seems to me very odd to be pillowed up in bed to write, but I have one of the funniest, sweetest and most cunning of babies. Although it is not a girl and at first I was disappointed, but now feel thankful for it is a boy. It is perfect in limb as can be and is a gift from God just as much as if it had been a girl. I have written a letter to his Aunt Clara and am getting tired now.

June 14, 1876

Sat up a few moments while my bed was being made, but felt glad enough to lie down again. The baby was dreadful cross last night and my sister-in-law was up almost the whole night with him. He has the colic and screeched like sixty. He is now asleep on the pillow beside me.

June 15, 1876

Had a great deal of company today. There were four girls in here at once and I talked and laughed so much Ma was afraid of a fever but I am feeling pretty strong and I'm getting along nicely. Weather very warm.

June 16, 1876

I was allowed to sit up an hour today and it seemed quite a rest from lying in bed. I read a piece in The Call, cut several blocks of patchwork and then went back to bed. Mrs. Freitas, Cora Levey, Mary Davids and Jennie Dolloff were here this afternoon. Mary brought a nice spring chicken for me to eat.

June 17, 1876

Saturday at last and Ruf is home. It seems so long from Monday till Saturday. But he is so tired after working all day that it would be hardly fair to expect him to come down often. The mill is running and all hands are at work.

The Good Templars had a grand picnic June 5th but I was sick at the time. They went to a place a mile this side of the Mill, Fairmont Park and enjoyed themselves very much.

June 18, 1876

Ruf is here. I am up with a rapper on as gay as you please. The baby is rigged up in his best clothes and was taken upstairs to see the borders. He is two weeks old today and I have been married 15 months today. I like to hear the church bells ring for they were ringing when he was born.

June 19, 1876

There was a great procession of Portuguese from the Catholic Church extending a full block. They carried a banner and the band of music played for them. It must have been some national holiday.

June 20, 1876

Weather warm and pleasant. Had a good many visitors today. Mrs. Stilson among the rest. Mrs. Lewis has started a dance school in her house, she has five young ladies to teach.

June 21, 1876

Warm today, there is to be a birthday party at Mrs. Guerrero's tonight and almost everybody has an invitation. Susie Miller the niece is 18 years old today.

June 22, 1876

Ma and father went to Moss Beach in the morning and bought a sack full of mosses so she is busy floating on tin and paper and I have not seen much of her today. Received a letter from Lottie Leach and one from Matilda Hariss. The weather is quite foggy.

June 23, 1876

Mr and Mrs. Heartly came back from the City today. They have been visiting schools for the last two weeks. There is quite a good deal of travel nowadays and the Hotel is full, weather warm.

June 24, 1876

The baby is so very cross. I have not had time to breathe and only caught a few moments to write in my Journal while Lil holds him, but it makes me so nervous.

June 25, 1876

The weather is warm. Lil and I took a nice walk. I left the baby at home asleep and Ma says she will put a white towel out the window if he wakes up. We went to the store on our way home and bought some nice peaches and candy.

June 26, 1876

I went to see Mrs. Lewis this morning and she was floating sea-moss as fast as she could. She wants to take it to the City tomorrow to give to Mrs. Boyd. Whether quite foggy and cold.

June 27, 1876

Ruf brought some splendid blackberries from the Mill and Ma is doing them up in bottles for me. Alvin is crying as loud as he can, he seems to have the colic most of the time.

June 28, 1876

Such a nice day I went to see Fannie Freitas. She was quite well and had some new things to show me that her sister had sent from Stockton. On my way home I stopped in to see the German woman and her baby has a "nudder toot."

June 29, 1876

Ruf took me out to ride. We left the baby at home and went as far as the toll gate. It was a very warm, pleasant day and I was well wrapped up so as not to catch cold. We met a good many who had not seen me since Alvin was born and they wanted to know what right we had to leave him at home.

June 30, 1876

The last day of June is very pleasant although it was a trifle foggy in the early morning. Miss Wolf made a real handsome sack for the baby. It is made of pink and white worsted and is pointed in the back like a breakfast cape. It fits him and looks so cunning.

July 1, 1876

People began to put up flags on their houses and stores today and on the Hotel there is a flag on each column of the porch and the large flag is flying from the top balcony. I declare, it looks quite patriotic.

July 2, 1876

Received two letters one from Cousin Mary asking me to send her some pieces of silk for her quilt she intends to call "Centennial." I suppose it would not do to make anything and not give it that name. The other letter was from Mrs. Price. She is now in Miss. She says it is such warm weather that people are dying by sun stroke and she almost melts there the climate is so different from California.

July 3, 1876

The folks are making great preparations for tomorrow as they expect a crowd of stage passengers to dinner. Received a letter from Clara telling about the Hay Makers party and one from Lizzie Anderson. She is visiting her mother in Mendocino and having a splendid time.

July 4, 1876

Father and Mother went to San Francisco this morning to see the parade. Ruf is here and is going to march with the Odd Fellows and to hear the oration. Mr. Campbell delivers it. They had a picnic too. The cannons were fired and flags in every direction. There is to be a ball in the evening in Pacific Hall.

July 5, 1876

Sent a dispatch to Ma this morning telling her everything was all right at home but she did not get it and being worried for fear things would go wrong she and father came home this evening. She brought a very pretty hat for baby trimmed with white ribbon and a sweet little brush for his hair. The brush is a present from Lil but she got Ma to buy it as she was in the City.

July 6, 1876

Ma has been telling us so much about the 4th of July in San Francisco that I can think of nothing else. The procession was such a grand affair she stood two hours on Montgomery Street looking at it. The streets were one mass of red, white and blue and everything bore the word "Centennial." The day was very warm and close. Ma met Mrs. Francis and Anna they want to see my baby very much.

July 7, 1876

Mrs. Lea has been here all the afternoon and I enjoyed her company very much. Fanny Freitas was here this evening till 10 o'clock. She was waiting for Mr. Freitas to close his store. I am writing this poorly but it is excusable for the baby is cross and I am holding him in one arm. The little rascal ought to be asleep.

July 19, 1876

Mrs. Lewis and Capt Boyd's wife came in the morning and stayed a long time. There was a great procession of Portuguese from the Catholic Church extending a full block. They carried a banner and the band of music played for them. It must have been some national holiday. I guess if I do not write better than this, I will deserve a bad mark but I can't help it.

July 31, 1876

I have been unable to write during the days that are missed here for I have suffered a great deal of pain with a sore breast. It had two leeches applied three times to keep the inflammation out. But it finally had to gather. It was probed yesterday and I find it much easier now. It pained so much that I could hardly raise my right arm. Lil took care of the baby most of the time and I do not know what I should have done without her. Cora Levie came and slept with me one night and washed the baby for me in the morning. Mrs. Sexton washed him once and Ellen did it the rest of the time. Ma is not feeling well. She has head ache and a boil on her left hip. It is very sore.

I think of going home to the Mill tomorrow. Maggie McGinty is going with me to help me work and clean up for I am not very strong yet and baby is very cross.

August 1, 1876

Here we are up in the redwoods. You can look north, south, east and west and see nothing but great trees. We came up in our new wagon and feel pretty tired after the jolting. Maggie got supper and we ate it with a relish.

August 2, 1876

Weather warm and very pleasant. I feel like a different person up here in the mountains and little Alvin has been real good all day. I do believe the change of climate has done him good for he laughs quite hearty this evening.

August 3, 1876

I heard today that Fannie Freitas has a big boy baby weighing nearly eleven pounds. I would like to see her and will go down soon. This has been another fine day, we did some house cleaning this morning.

August 4, 1876

Maggie and I have been very busy all day. We cleaned the pantry, put new papers on the shelves, washed the dishes that have been standing so long and scrubbed the floor. We found it quite a job. Alvin was a good baby so I did not have to leave my work to take care of him. It seems that the climate agrees with him.

August 5, 1876

Delightful weather. We had a shower this morning and did not see the sun till ten o'clock but when it came up it was warm and nice. We cleaned the kitchen, washed windows and brushed down cobwebs of which there was plenty and to spare.

August 6, 1876

On the seventh day we rested. It has been very pleasant today and we have been sitting around reading and tending baby. I gathered a magnificent bouquet from our garden and sent it to Lil as she is so fond of flowers. We have some wine colored dahlias and some lemon colored. Very pretty and a good variety of 4 o'clocks. Our pinks have been destroyed by gophers.

August 7, 1876

Ruf sent to San Francisco for a case of porter for me to drink on account of the baby and I do not have milk enough. So I will have to start and drink it although I do not like the taste for it is bitter. The case holds eight dozen bottles so you see I have the chance of becoming a regular tosser before I get through the case. Weather continues fine. Ma is not so well, she has sprained her back and is unable to sit up.

August 8, 1876

There just as I take a pen in hand I hear a little squeal from my bedroom so I suppose it means "Come and take me up for I am awake." So I will only write a few words. The day has been warm, Ruf is making a crib for baby out of curled wood.

August 9, 1876

Nice day. We did some washing this morning and ironing in the afternoon so we feel pretty tired. I want to go home and see the folks tomorrow so I worked quite hard. Ruf is at the Mill. Mrs. Lewis, Jennie Dolloff, Miss Wiggins and Abe Nichols were up here. They brought lunch with them picnic style and then called to see me.

August 10, 1876

Got up early this morning, gave baby a hasty bath, made my bed, dressed and was ready before Ruf was so I stood at the gate while he harnessed Prince and Tib. We found Ma in bed but relieved of her pain a little. Lil had been rubbing her back with turpentine and as it is so penetrating Ma was afraid to use much of it. We stayed till three o'clock and drove home in good season. Maggie had a nice hot supper ready so it tasted good to us.

August 11, 1876

Been cleaning the parlor and spare bedroom. It took some time for I have so many trinkets on the whatnot that it is tedious to fix them. My rustic shelf is another bother. It has wood moss on it, then seashells, pinecones, Pescadero pebbles, pressed wild flowers and some specimens of Salt Lake City minerals. My piano and guitar have not been touched yet.

August 12, 1876

Just as Maggie and I were cleaning the dining room we heard a knock at the door. It was Dr. McCarty and Cora Levie. Cora has been sitting up at night with her sick sister and was completely worn out. She had been vaccinated the week before and took cold in her arm so it was very much inflamed and she was half sick herself. We got lunch for them and I then insisted on Cora lying down in my bed to rest. She did so and is still there. I will try to keep her all night.

August 13, 1876

A pleasant but sad day. Dr. Gurdy came up this morning to tell Cora that her sister was dead. She had brain fever and became paralyzed in her limbs besides. She was in great agony till death relieved her. She was married and leaves a husband and three children one a baby of two weeks.

August 14, 1876

Ruf and Maggie went to Mrs. McDougall's funeral. I could not go very far with a baby. The day was so foggy and damp. She was buried in the Odd Fellows ground, the first laid there and now she sleeps alone. It seems so sad and dreary but soon more will follow.

August 15, 1876

Another sad, sad day. Ruf came home from the Mill at three o'clock and told us James was dead. How sudden it was! They were splitting logs and he fell between two of them crushing the breath out of his body in less than a minute. All the men stood by and saw the terrible accident. They rolled the logs apart as soon as they could but he only gasped once or twice.

Ruf says he never saw such a sight before and does not want to witness another. They sent for a doctor immediately, but could do no good. James was a man we all liked. He worked for Father a year ago and had only been working for Ruf a few months. He has a mother in England, she is seventy six years old and I fear the blow will kill her.

August 16, 1876

Ma wrote to her and sent a lock of his hair. The Free Masons of which he was a member, had him buried from their Hall. He had a very large funeral for he had many friends. Alice Felt, a young lady that he though a great deal of, went in black for him. He is the first one laid in the Mason's ground and only the day before he died he remarked at the funeral of Mrs. McDougall, "Well she is alone but I may soon be near her." Little did he know how soon without one moment's notice.

August 17, 1876

I hardly think of anything to write for my mind has been so sad all day. It seems but an hour since James was here in this very room, holding my baby as he did last Sunday morning, in full health and glee and now to be gone, but such is life. Today we are here, but tomorrow where? Echo answers where? I forgot to say that my brother's wife from Gilroy is here, she came on the 13th and brought her three children.

August 18, 1876

O, what a racket, what a noise three children make. They upset everything inside and outside of the house. Gertie is 6, Eugene 4 and Milton 2 years old, so they are all small and keep their mother running for them all day. First one wants something to eat, then another has fallen in the water and a third has got hurt, so it goes all day. Maggie and I feel almost crazy. This morning they knocked all the pears off the trees and turned the chicken boxes over, and then came in with their eyes and ears full of sawdust. Annie folded her arms and looked at them saying, "The Lord help us!" I think it is enough to drive one mad to take charge of three young ones.

August 19, 1876

Weather foggy and very gloomy. There was a picnic in the woods just below our house and a good many were there from town. Lil came up with Mrs. Lewis and quite a number came over to see us. After lunch we walked down to the ground to give the children a change. I took my baby but Lil would not allow me to hold him a minute she was so glad to see him. The day was so cold people did not enjoy a ramble through the woods. But they had dancing and music by the Catholic Band. It was not quite right to have a picnic so soon after two funerals but it is the way of the world.

August 20, 1876

This has been a real nice day and I wanted to go down to church very much but it was out of the question to do so for if I got up at daylight and got the baby dressed, breakfast over and myself ready we would then be too late for service by the time we would reach town. So I have to abandon the idea as long as we remain in the woods which I hope will not be forever.

August 21, 1876

So this was washday and we are all tired. I guess I will find but little to write except soap suds and a basket of clean clothes.

August 22, 1876

Quite a warm day. We did our ironing this morning and in the afternoon Annie and Maggie went over to the orchard across the creek to get some apples and plums. The children are waiting for some very patiently.

August 23, 1876

Weather gloomy again. Maggie finished a pretty wrapper for me today. It is made of brown and white calico, has a ruffle around the bottom and pocket. I made a new kitchen apron from Madame Demorest's pattern and Annie made a new apron for Gertie, so we were in the sewing business. I like to sew dull days.

August 24, 1876

Heard today that Ma is not so well and I will go down on Saturday to stay overnight. Warmer weather today, a man came with fruit. I bought a box of peaches, some sweet potatoes and eating apples.

August 25, 1876

Warm today and we took a walk after ferns. Found a great many nice ones, also some fine maiden's hair for hanging baskets.

Alice Felt and Laura McGinty were up to sell tickets for a fair for the benefit of the Methodist Church. They want to pay the debt. The girls sold quite a number at the sawmill. The men did not want to go but they wanted to help.

August 26, 1876

Came down this afternoon about three o'clock. Found Ma very sick and unable to move in bed. She does not have much appetite and I cooked her a leg of chicken but she ate a very little. Fannie Freitas came over to see me and Mrs. Stilson and Mrs. Jewell also called this afternoon. I must now undressed Alvin.

August 27, 1876

Ruf went home today but said that I might stay till Tuesday as Ma was feeling so bad so I am here still. Ellen my sister-in-law was taken sick in the afternoon and I went to see her. She was too sick to leave so I stayed with her and about seven o'clock, while the church bell was ringing, she had a little baby boy. Wesley and Dr. McGoudy were there and I took the little stranger and washed and dressed it. So cunning it is and so fat. I came home shortly after for her mother came on the stage.

August 28, 1876

Ma is better this evening. Mrs. Nichols is sitting with her and Mrs. Lea has just gone home. Lil is holding Alvin for he is a little cross. The day has been cold and gloomy

Received a letter from Lizzie and one from Cousin Mary.

August 29, 1876

Came home to the Mill today. Father brought me in the buggy. The wind blew very hard and we were covered with dust. The poor baby had to have his head covered up all the time for the air would have taken his breath away. I found all well up here and they seem to be glad to see me back again. Brought some candy and peanuts for the children.

August 30, 1876

Had quite a time this morning putting things straight after being away and in the afternoon helped to make a pique wrapper for baby. It is white and has a canton flannel[9] back. I trimmed it with embroidery and it looks real sweet. Annie did the Machine sewing on it. I also cut and made a bib for him.

---

[9] Canton flannel or cotton flannel is napped on one side or two side.

September 1, 1876

Ruth, Annie, Maggie, three children, baby and myself all came down to the Hotel today. Maggie went to see her mother and Annie and the children took the one o'clock stage for San Mateo, then the cars for Hollister. I am to stay down two days. Ma is now able to sit up and I am so glad.

September 2, 1876

Nice weather Ellen is getting along nicely, her baby is real good. Only had the colic once or twice. Ma is feeling better. Lil went to the fair last night and bought a china match-safe for me. It is such a funny ornament, it represents two cats and an owl sitting upon the music book looking at them. She said she ate so much ice cream that she was most froze.

September 3, 1876

Home again. How quiet the house is after the children are gone. We got home in time to get supper before dark and get Alvin ready for bed. We came in the wagon and as there was not much weight we got shook up a good deal.

Annie McGinty came back with Maggie to stay a few days as the school has vacation for a week.

September 4, 1876

So rainy today we did not wash so we made a sewing day of it. Annie found a nest of eggs in the bushes by the side of the creek. It had seven eggs in it. Rather dull here today. Ruf has just got home.

September 5, 1876

Brighter but not very much sun today. We washed in the morning but the clothes did not dry till late in the afternoon and some of them are left out all night. Some of the pears fell from our trees and we had baked pears for supper.

September 6, 1876

Nice sunny day. I starched the baby's clothes and got them dry very quick. Then ironed while Maggie was cooking supper. We had sweet potatoes and oyster soup. Ruf finished the crib for Alvin today. It is a real neat piece of work and the headboard is of curled wood.

September 7, 1876

This has been a very warm day. Maggie and I have been putting up peaches all today. We had two boxes and it took some time to peel and half them, weigh and cook them and get them finished. I had to work half of the time with the baby on my knee for it always happens that if a person wants to do anything particular, it will be just the time the baby is cross. Annie went home today. I gave her three aprons that were too short for me.

September 8, 1876

Ruf and Mr. Borden went to Redwood City today on a law suit I believe and did not get home till quite late, so Maggie milked the cow and fed the calf and I shut the chicken boxes up and collected the eggs. We get nine or ten everyday now. But, it won't last long, for the hens will all want to set at once.

September 9, 1876

Weather pretty fair. Ruf wanted to go down town to the Lodge this evening but changed his mind when the time came to saddle the horse. I think he was too tired for he had been chopping down trees in the creek in front of the house so that we can see the road very plain now and it is so much company to see the teams pass.

September 10, 1876

Ruf went to town and took two of the men with him. Maggie and I got our morning work done as soon as we could. Then we sat out on the porch with the baby and our books. Dan Galligher went hunting for a deer on the summit, but as he could not get it, he shot quails on the way home and gave us seven for supper. Ruf brought some melons and a big paper of candies for me.

September 11, 1876

We have been moving today that is I changed my sleeping room to one nearer the kitchen so that when the baby wakes I can hear him cry. We had a number of things to move and curtains to tack up and it took all the morning. This has been an extremely warm day.

September 12, 1876

Wash day again. It seems to roll around pretty fast and there was not a particle of sun out to dry the clothes. I was sorry we did not wash yesterday, the weather is so changeable this time of year.

September 13, 1876

Starching, ironing, and sewing were the order of exercises for today and we had a good deal of each to do. Fancy things for the baby took time to fix. Maggie is sewing on a new dress for me. It is gray and intended for traveling. The polonaise[10] is small gray and black plaid, all wool and to be trimmed with fringe and small buttons.

September 14, 1876

We took a walk to the Mill this afternoon. It was very dusty and we did not enjoy it much for we had to take turns in carrying baby and had to hold our dresses out of the dirt. We saw two snakes across the path. When we got to the mill they were oiling the machinery so we took a ride on the car. We went to the end of the road which is little over half mile and the view (as the car turns around on the road) is beautiful. Mr. Borden offered to carry Alvin back but we would not let him, so we walked back to the Mill and found them all at work. Ruf was sawyer and had on a log five feet in diameter. Dave was tending the brakes and Mr. Barnard was edging the lumber. It made such a frightful noise, we were glad to come away, I got four letters today, one from Cavendish, Vt. And one from Matilda Hauss telling of her success in the examination and her obtaining a Second Grade certificate. I was real glad to hear it.

---

[10] Polonaise: a garment of the 1870's and 1880's revival style consisting of a gown with a cutaway, draped and swaggered overskirt, worn over a petticoat.

September 15, 1876

Gloomy weather. Maggie washed several pieces but could not get them dry. Everything seems so dull and quiet that it makes me feel stupid. I have been mending some of Ruf's clothes and washing my head in vinegar and water which was not a wise thing to do when the weather is damp. Laura McGinty came and staid a couple of hours with us. She rode horseback.

September 16, 1876

We expected to go to a picnic today to be given by the Spanish in honor of their independence, but unfortunately the weather was so rainy they had to postpone it.

September 17, 1876

Ruf went after bees today or rather after honey but when he got stung three times, he gave it up as a bad job and came home. He was awake all night with tooth ache so he has retired early for it is only seven o'clock now. Weather still gloomy.

September 18, 1876

We went down to see the folks at home today. Of course it was wash day but I could not resist when Ruf mentioned about going home. It was a very warm day but the roads were good on account of yesterday's dampness. We found them all well, Ma was able to go downstairs and to work a little. Lil is making three bibs for Alvin. Received a letter from brother William and a splendid long one from Clara full of news and I feel so "chirked up"[11] I want to sit right down and answer it. She says Emma Holden is to be married today.

September 19, 1976

Washed and ironed today. The sun was so hot I got my arms and hands as brown as a gypsy's hanging the clothes out. I put up a box of large white grapes and expect you will be here sometime to help me put them down. O dear, I put some perfumed hair oil on my hair today and it has been coaxing the flies ever since so keep brushing at them while I write.

September 20, 1876

Another unpleasant day. I declare I never saw such weather as we have been enjoying. First one nice warm day when we dress to suit and the next day, put on a thick waterproof and not be too warm.

Alice Wolf and Mary Davids came up to see us and spend the day. They started from town at nine o'clock and were three hours on the road. They say the horse acted mean and wanted to turn round all the time, so they did not reach here till twelve. Then we had dinner

---

[11] Chirked up: cheer up or inspire.

and they stayed till three o'clock and allowed three hours more to go home in so they will hail up at supper time. It only takes an hour to go with a decent horse. Alice is making baby another sack. It is salmon and white.

Ruf is sawing today. He got up at five o'clock and will not be home till late. I have five letters to write so I must be about them.

September 21, 1876

I have been flying around like water off a grindstone today: for tomorrow is Ruf's birthday and we want to give him a real nice dinner. So I made a custard pie (his favorite dish) and Maggie and I spent a whole hour trying to catch a chicken we finally caught and were part of another hour in killing the poor thing. Weather nice and pleasant.

September 22, 1876

We spent a very pleasant day. Father and Ma came up in the buggy and staid all day on account of it being Ruf's birthday. We had a very nice dinner for the occasion and Ruf came down from the Mill to eat. He was sawing so he could not stay long. Father brought him a large box of cigars and Ma made two mince pies for him. They found the road very dusty.

September 23, 1876

Saturday, especially when it is clear and bright, always brings its' work with it so Maggie and I have been working around the door way washing the porch and a few articles for baby which have to be attended to whether it is a wet or dry day. In the afternoon Ruf went down to the Lodge and will not be home till midnight for it will be dark and he has a long ride so I will play Piano till I am tired and then read as long as I can hold my eyes open. I have sixteen literary magazines. I sent to Boston for them, gave one dollar in greenback and got back numbers. Maggie is writing to Ida Rock.

September 24, 1876

Ruf got home at 10 o'clock last night and told me that Ellen was suffering very much with a gathered breast[12] so he took me down to see her today and I felt very sorry indeed. She is not able to raise her hand and in great pain. I can fully sympathize with her for I know how it is from experience. Nice warm day, got back home at 6 o'clock.

September 25, 1876

Got a couple of letters today. Washed this morning and the weather was so warm the clothes were dry in

---

[12] Gathered Breast: an absolute term for breast abscess or cellulitis of the breast.

no time. Maggie is finishing my new dress. I sent to the City by Mrs. Lewis to get the buttons for it.

September 26, 1876

Got up early and starched the baby's clothes so as to iron them in the afternoon. Made bread and cake, had green corn and sweet potatoes for supper. Alvin has been real good, he is crowing a squealing now but he ought to be in bed. Mr. Borden comes in almost every night to sing to baby and that is what keeps him awake. He has been singing "Old Zip Coon"[13] and "Dan Tucker" to him.

September 27, 1876

Went visiting today to see a neighbor, Mrs. Markman, who lives about a mile from here. We started to walk and carry baby but when we had gone but little way we overtook a lumber wagon going from the Mill and asked a ride. I was soon mounted on top of a big high seat with my feet swinging and baby on my arm and a big Portuguese man beside me. Quite romantic wasn't it? But better than walking in the dust. We were made very welcome by Mrs. Markman and enjoyed a splendid dinner prepared by her and ate so much we were obliged to loosen our belts. We came home late in the afternoon. Mr. Markman brought us in his wagon and she gave me some nice large cucumbers and ripe pears.

---

[13] "Old Zip Coon" written in 1834 is known today as "Turkey in the Straw."

September 28, 1876

As we were off all day yesterday we had to start in fresh and work with a will today. We had a few pieces of ironing to do in the morning. Ruf is working in the redwoods today. Some of his men were blasting and set the woods on fire. It burned a good deal of lumber but will be watched all night for fear of scattering the fire.

September 29, 1876

There was quite a shower of rain about four o'clock this morning and it has been very gloomy weather all day. The roads will be improved, but it is bad for the new mines and Ruf did not welcome the rain for he has an interest in the mine. Besides the farmers are not quite ready for rain, but, we must take it when God sees fit to send it and be satisfied. We should be like the man who said the morrow would be just such weather as pleased him because it would please God, and said he, "What pleases God, pleases me."

September 30, 1876

Very busy today, getting ready to go to San Jose. We are making cake to take with us. Father, Ma, Ruf and I intend to go in the wagon and drive Tib and Prince all the way. I suppose it will be quite tiresome to hold baby but as he is generally so good he will be but little trouble.

October 1, 1876

As this is Sunday and we cannot go to Church we spent the day very quietly sitting on the porch reading. Baby was contented to lie on a quilt and pillow and kick his feet in the sun. Watch and the cat were lying there asleep and altogether it was a peaceful scene.

> Another day its course has run,
> And still O God thy child is blest,
> For thou hast been by day my sun,
> And then will be by night my rest.

October 2, 1876

Washing took up most of our time today for I tried to get everything done up clean as I hate to go away and leave an article not clean. I have a letter to write so must hurry as Ruf says he will not allow me to sit up late.

October 3, 1876

Ironing, third of the day, sewing another third and

packing up the rest of the time. Maggie was trying to finish my traveling dress, so I helped her. I made forty button holes and sewed eighty buttons on. I think that is enough for one day. I declare everything I look at resembles buttons. Tomorrow we are off for Spanish Town so as to be ready to start next day on our trip.

October 4, 1876

We came down home this morning about eleven o'clock after getting the work done and house nicely cleaned up. I worked so long on my dress last night that when I got asleep I dreamed some man was trying to shoot me with little buttons and that I escaped by jumping through a button hole.

Ma is all ready to start and we have to get up about five tomorrow morning, so good night, let fleas bite, snore with all your might.

October 5, 1876

Father routed us out of bed before daylight and although I was anxious to go I must say it came pretty tough to get out of a nice, warm bed so early; especially when nothing but a heavy fog greets your eyes, as was the case on the coast. But, I gave a bound and landed in the middle of the room, dressed myself and baby in a jiffy and after taking a cup of coffee we were soon on the road. When we reached San Mateo, the sun was shining brightly, so we took our time and got to Menlo Park just at noon. We ate our lunch under a large oak and enjoyed it very much. We went to a neighboring house to get a drink, walked around a little to get the cramp out of our knees, then resumed our journey.

Bought a watermelon of a man who had a wagon load of them. Stopped under a tree at Mountain View and ate it while sitting in the wagon. It tasted refreshing I tell you, and we went on after giving the horses water and did not stop till we arrived at San Jose. We washed the dust off our faces, gave baby a bath, dressed him nice and clean and went down to supper at five o'clock. Didn't we make good time?

October 6, 1876

Got up pretty late as we were tired and needed rest. Took breakfast, went for a ride along the principal streets. I never enjoyed anything so much for there are so many nice trees to ride under from San Jose to Santa Clara and a little beyond. How I should like to live here or just out of town a few miles. Ruf wants to look at some places with the intentions of buying when he sells out the Mill.

October 7, 1876

Went to the fair last evening. Took baby, he was delighted with the gas light and so many people he hardly knew what to do. I saw many very old articles that were on exhibition, one quilt in particular that belonged to an old lady there. It was an autograph, and had verses and names of such men as Henry Clay, Webster, Fillmore and many others. It was quilted in many designs and very fine stitches. We stayed till 11 o'clock and Father carried Alvin to the Hotel for me. We stopped at the "Exchange." Mr. Barker, Proprietor.

October 8, 1876

Got up at 6 o'clock and walked around a little. Could not go to Church with baby. Mrs. Cook came last evening on the cars, she has a friend here. Ma, Ruf and I went to see Ellen Johnston. She is living here at present. Her sisters Hannah and Jeanette are attending the Normal School[14] and Ellen is keeping house for them. She wants Lil to come and stay a week and Ma will let her come as soon as we get back home.

October 9, 1876

Started for home this morning at 1/2 7 o'clock (there I've got that wrong end foremost.) Brought lunch with us and ate at Mayfield. Had some nice grapes and delicious apples also. Did not get out of the wagon to rest. Brought Mrs. Cook with us as far as San Mateo. Reached home before dark well pleased with our few days of absence. I say home but you will have to pay attention for I have two homes now and

---

[14] Normal School: an institution created to train teachers. During the 19th century in the United States, instruction in normal schools was at the high school level, turning out primary school teachers.

we are at Father's tonight. Baby stood the change first rate. No crying at all.

October 10, 1876

Came home to the redwoods this afternoon and have been busy putting away things ever since. I bought a number of things for the baby as I intend to put him in short clothes when he is five months old. I bought six pairs of woolen stockings, one pair of ankle ties, bronze, one pair leggings, material for three dresses, one pink and white plaid, one blue and white and one scarlet cashmere, three woolen shirts, just as cunning as they can be and flannel for a nice skirt that I intend to embroider so I will now have plenty of sewing to do.

October 11, 1876

Lots of long clothes in the wash today and such a pile of ironing as I will have for tomorrow. Is enough to give one fever and ague[15] but I will have to take my time for tucks and embroidery cannot be hurried. Maggie is busy clearing off the supper table and now the baby calls my attention. Ruf is milking the cow.

---

[15] Ague: a fit of shivering or shaking or successive states of chills and fever that is a symptom of malaria.

Maria Jane Schuyler Hatch

October 12, 1876

After ironing a few pieces I gave baby a bath and while he was asleep I cut out a little dress and almost made it before night. But I sat so steady that I feel sick so I will take a bath and go to bed early. We have a great many nice flowers in the garden and a bouquet on the table here smells so fragrant mostly cloth of gold roses.

October 13, 1876

Slight rain this morning and heavier in the afternoon. Read a letter from Cousin Robert describing the Great Centennial, he went to the exhibition at Philadelphia. In one part of his letter he says the most he can say is like the country girl who went to the Exhibition and wrote home,

Dear Ma,
I've been to the big show. 0000000.
Your loving daughter,
Sarah Jane Jenkins.

He says a person cannot describe half he sees. He was looking very earnest at something when all at once he felt someone come down on his favorite corn, (the one he had raised on purpose for the Centennial,) and when he looked down he saw a number 12 boot belonging to a big stout granger. He made the exclamation Je ru sa lem and the granger looked at him as unconcerned as you please. He makes a comical sketch of it all the way through. Says he went there with a pocket full of money and a paper collar and came back without a dime and was welcomed at the station by a grand serenade consisting of one small boy playing a trumpet assisted by another boy same size blowing a fish horn.[16] His friends were so glad to hear of his return that they gave him a grand dinner of cod fish and potatoes mashed down with weak tea. He thinks he was highly honored and while he was in Philadelphia the only annoyance he felt was being taken for Don Pedro, Henry Ward Beacher[17] and Don Carlos. He says all the women who had children there wanted him to stand Godfather for them. He wrote such a big letter it cost him Fifteen cents to send it.

October 14, 1876

We have been house cleaning today, sweeping parlor and spare bedroom and arranging my what - not. It is a big job in itself. I have one shelf for books, one for rustic such as H M Bay shells, Pescadero pebbles, minerals from Salt Lake City and Nevada pine cones from Yosemite, sea moss from Santa Barbara, tree moss from these Redwoods, autumn leaves from Vermont and a few large shells from Mexico. Now don't you think that a variety for one shelf? Yes and I have a Hickory nut from Wilton

---

[16] Fish Horn: a horn that produces a loud and penetrating sound, used by a fishmonger to announce that the catch is in.
[17] Henry Ward Beecher 1813-1887 was an American Congregationalist, clergyman, social reformer and speaker known for his support of the abolition of slavery and his emphasis on God's love.

Connecticut, a nut from China and one from Minnesota that Ruf has cut into a small basket. Then I have a shelf of cabinet photographs. I have 42 of them, all are friends of mine.

October 15, 1876

Another Sabbath. We got up early and started for Spanishtown but we were too late for church. I wanted to hear the new minister very much. His name is Mr. Todd, he has a wife who is East at present but she intends to return soon and get music scholars in town as she is quite a musician I understand.

Lil went to church, she and Ma go every evening of service and they like the sermons very much.

October 16, 1876

There has been a very hard rain today enough to make the roads bad for a month. Ruf went to the Mill today and got his clothing very wet. It rains so hard I can't write.

October 17, 1876

O' dear what can the matter be? Our clothes didn't get washed you see, and no telling when they will get done either if the rain continues. My dining room has a porch and low windows and it looks terrible gloomy and dark. I went to play Piano to chirk me up and behold the young one set up a scream and drowned all my fine music, so I gave up in despair and after laying him on a pillow on his stomach I grabbed my Journal thinking to tell it all my troubles and find comfort.

October 18, 1876

Well, I do believe the sun intends to stay in the shade altogether. If so I am doomed to be as cloudy as the weather. Baby has his nose stopped up with cold in the head. Maggie has her back up about something, Ruf has his boots on the stove to dry and I have my domain up on the table writing, so we are are all up in the world, can you give a fit recipe to get us all down?

October 19, 1876

Did not rain today but began to smile as if the sun was ashamed to play hide and seek so long. It only just peeked at us a little but it did us a minute of good. I ran for the dirty clothes, Ruf put the boiler on and Maggie got wash tubs out in a twinkling. So we managed to get the washing out but not a thread got dry. Still a little bleaching will do them good, and we will hope for sun on the morrow.

October 20, 1876

Got clothes partly dry, ironed them and have them to air. Mrs. McGinty and Annie came up in their buggy to stay a couple of days with us. I suppose they thought we would be lonely up here in this weather. I was glad to have them come. The wind is blowing hard now. Lil's birthday. I gave her a birdcage.

October 21, 1876

Been very busy sewing all day. Maggie took her mother and sister up to the new saw mill this afternoon. They were gone two hours. I am making a white apron for Alvin gored and the seams corded with blue calico, very pretty. And I also made a linen shirt with inserting and edge of hair pin crochet.

October 22, 1876

A nice warm day. I always like Sunday to be pleasant for it is always so quiet that it seems nice to have it sunny. Mrs. McGinty and Annie went home this afternoon and it seems real quiet without them for we talked a great deal while they were here.

October 23, 1876

The people of H.M.B. are talking about the Catholic Fair. It commences tomorrow night and will continue three nights. We are all going the last night, if the weather is fine and nothing prevents. Made a dress for baby and finished six flannel skirts for him. It is quite a task to make the skirts, for each must have buttons and button-holes and straps and it takes some time. Besides I like to put something on the hem of each. I have seven white skirts to make this week and ever so many aprons for future sewing.

October 24, 1876

Maggie did the work while I sewed for I am anxious to get a good many clothes made before I put the baby in short ones so that I will have enough if it rains or if I should not have a chance to make more soon. Made a neat brilliant apron trimmed with embroidery and a linen with pink spots in it that Ma gave me.

October 25, 1876

Have not been able to do much today for baby had an attack of colic and demanded my whole attention. Ruf has been cutting down some of the poplar trees in the creek in front of the door and we can now see the road quite plain.

October 26, 1876

Hurried and got through our work, dressed and went to town to attend the fair in the evening. It was held in Pacific Hall and was crowded. They had a good many nice things to see and some to raffle. They had a hobby horse, the largest in the United States. It was a large as a common sized pony and took up lots of room. Ruf took three chances on a horse blanket and won it. He took a chance on a large fruitcake and won that. I had two dollars worth of chances, but won nothing, and ran home with my tail between my legs like a frightened pup.

The band played well. I came home early.

October 27, 1876

Came back to the mill this afternoon. Maggie has a bad cold and feels miserable after sitting up so late last night at the fair. She was with Ida Rockefeller. I ate some ice cream at the fair and the baby feels the effect of it today for he is uncommon cross and I had to give him a dose of peppermint to ease him.

October 28, 1876

Fannie Freitas came up to spend a few days with me. She brought her baby. He is a big fat fellow, weighs sixteen pounds and looks twice as large as Alvin. He is a perfect chunk and cries most of the time. Fannie is trying to break him into going to sleep without rocking as I do with Alvin. I lay him in the crib and he sucks his thumb till he falls asleep.

October 29, 1876

Lil lost her pet canary. It seems the bottom of the cage I gave her came unfastened and fell and the bird flew away. She was taking a buggy ride at the time and when she came back could not find her bird. I feel sorry because I gave the cage and she might not have lost her bird in the old cage. Ruf just came home from town. Fannie is undressing her baby and my little scrub[18] demands my attention.

October 30, 1876

Fannie and I gave our babies their bath and put them to bed. Then we helped Maggie with the washing. I rinsed and Fannie hung the clothes up. All done before noon and sewed in the afternoon. Fannie basted six muslin shirts for her baby and I stitched them on the machine for her. So we did quite a lot of sewing. Weather rainy today I am afraid it will rain hard all night and the clothes will get a double rinse.

October 31, 1876

Bright again. Fannie went home I guess she intended to stay longer but was afraid it would rain and she could not get home. I went down in the wagon with her and Ruf. Ate dinner at home and came back here in the evening. Found the house warm and dinner almost ready.

---

[18] Scrub: a person who mooches off others.

November 1, 1876

The melancholy days have come: the saddest of the year and why so? It is because the trees are bare and flowers cease to bloom? If so we still have beauties left for now we may gather our beautiful autumn leaves and tree mosses and decorate our walls to keep us from feeling gloomy and to occupy our time. Then we have more leisure to write and read and improve our minds instead of visiting around.

November 2, 1876

Received a letter from Capt. Francis. He wishes me to pay them another visit and I should like very much to go. Ruf says I may go if I can get along with the baby. If I get his short clothes made I will venture I guess. Anna wrote from School in Oakland wanting to see baby. I suppose she will make a great fuss over him when she sees him.

November 3, 1876

Been sewing all day. Made three little aprons, one

pink calico trimmed with a tulip vine you gave me, another white cross bar with embroidery and third white, corded and bound with blue chambra. All are very pretty and although some work to make, are a credit to the lady who made them (ahem!) My eyes begin to blink so I shall say good night, sleep and dream you and I are eating ice cream.

November 4, 1876

Alvin is five months old today and I rigged him up in short clothes. He does look so cute. I declare it would make a cat laugh to see him. He has such short legs that his stockings run clear up his back and he looks like a prize monkey dressed to run with an organ grinder. He is so attracted with his shoes, (bronze ankle ties) that he cannot keep his eyes off them and is glad his feet have more liberty.

November 5, 1876

Went home today and found Ma quite sick with another carbuncle. This is a large one on her left hip and more painful than the rest were, she seems to suffer very much and the Doctor says it is serious to have so many. She uses flaxseed poultices hot three or four times a day to ease it. I stayed right by her all day and did not come home till near dark.

November 6, 1876

Washed and ironed today and feel pretty tired. Alvin was quite cross on account of a dose of castor oil I gave him so I had to stop and pet him between times.

November 7, 1876

All are snuggly tucked into bed except me and I did not dare throw off on my old friend Journal for fear Clara would know it and call me lazy but I did want to go when I saw the rest make tracks. The weather is very fine and I hope it will continue so for I have decided to go to the City next week if all is well and it is so hard to get disappointed, especially when a baby is to be traveling companion, one has to go in fair weather. A great many children are dying this winter from diphtheria and the paper states new cases of smallpox. Election day and noisy streets.

November 8, 1876

Been sewing very steady today. Did not take time to practice. Ruf says if I slight my music he will send the piano away so I shall have to be careful and strike up a tune when he is around. Alvin was as good as pie today. He sat in a chair half the time and lay on his back on the sofa kicking his heels up the other half, so his Mama had a good time to sew. Weather clear.

November 9, 1876

Thursday again and sweeping, baking in the morning and in the afternoon a drive down to see how Ma is. She is much better but thinks she will have to suffer with another carbuncle as a very small red spot begins to show itself just above the large one and that will make 25 she has had. I pity her from my heart and wish I could relieve her.

November 10, 1876

No fish for today. What shall we do? Friday comes but once a week and then we have no fish. I guess I must open a box of sardines or cook some codfish for supper. Good weather yet. Guess we shall have a dry winter.

November 11, 1876

Mr. Borden has been here all the evening, playing with baby. The little fellow knows him and crows to him while he sits on Mr. Borden's knee. Maggie is reading a book and Ruf is talking.

November 12, 1876
Millville (small home near the lumber mill)

Sunday again and no chance to go to Church. I sometimes feel as though my lot was cast in a hard place for while others are so situated that they can attend Church and do not care about going, here I am (who was raised in Sunday School from the time I was four years old) deprived of the pleasure of hearing a Sermon on the Sabbath. When I murmur Ruf says, "O well, we will not always live in the woods. Weather pleasant, health good so we ought to be thankful."

November 13, 1876

Washing, ironing, sewing and election talk takes up today and evening. It seems undecided which will gain the field; Tilden is said to be elected and many of the citizens of our beloved town got intoxicated in honor of the event, but later news is that it is impossible to decide as yet. Ruf is on the Republican side and father is strong Democrat so when we are at home we hear a strong argue and of course both think their side will lead. Ruf ran for County Supervisor but was beaten by Judge Ames. He does not feel very bad over it however, for he had not made up his mind to run till a few days before the election.

November 14, 1876
Spanishtown

Very busy sewing all day. Baby has been very good and so cunning. He claps his hand for "pat- a-cake" just as nice as he can. I am almost ready for my trip to the City. Shall leave here on Wednesday and will remain away near two weeks. Maggie promises to stay and keep house and have her sister Laura with her till my return.

November 15, 1876

Left the Mill about nine o'clock this morning after giving Alvin a bath as usual. At two o'clock we attended the funeral of Mr. McDougall, a neighbor of ours. He was killed by running to stop his team. It seems he had got off his wagon to bid goodbye to a friend and had neglected to put the brake on the wagon. The horses became frightened and in running to stop them, he slipped and the wagon passed over him, killing him instantly. It is just three months since he buried his wife. His funeral took place from Odd Fellows Hall and was largely attended. This afternoon I packed my valise for traveling. Baby is now asleep and I will put my hair up and go to bed that I may feel bright on the morrow. It looks very much like rain tonight and it really had the impudence to sprinkle a little.

November 16, 1876
San Mateo

Got up pretty good season and made a rush for the window to see if it had been raining. To my dismay it was pouring down hard and Ruf poked his head up from the bed and said, "Well old lady, I guess San Mateo nor, any other "San" won't see you today." O said I, it may clear up, but, my heart sank below zero.

However, if "disappointment sinks the heart, the renewal of hope gives consolation." So I kept an eye on the weather all the morning and it began to look brighter at noon and although the family and Ruf thought I ought not venture, I did start on the stage at one o'clock and am now in San Mateo visiting Mrs. Tilton till tomorrow. She was glad to see me. Also to see baby who was a stranger to her. We have been chatting ever since we met and are likely to keep it up for I am to sleep with Mrs. Tilton tonight. Ella is playing piano now. Miss Haas called to see me this evening. There, your young nephew is calling me from the other room and if I do not answer he will show his lungs off to advantage. I want him to show his good qualities while away from home so good night, out with your light.

November 17, 1876
San Francisco

Did not sleep well last night for not being used to sleeping three in a bed. I was anxious about baby for fear he might smother, but at daylight I took a peep at him and he was alright. After breakfast I gave baby a bath, washed his napkins and hung them by the stove as the sun was not very strong and the ground was damp then Mrs. Tilton, Ella and myself took a stroll around her garden and grounds near the house, plucked a bouquet of choice flowers and when tired went back to the house. Found baby still asleep sweetly, had lunch, played a tune, read the poem Elaine, fed baby and prepared to leave on the 2 o'clock train for the City. Ella went to the depot with me. I arrived in the City at 3:20 and got off the train on Valencia Street. Took horse cars for Seventeenth and walked two blocks to Capp Street. I was fortunate enough to meet a kind gentleman who, seeing that I was overburdened, offered and did carry my satchel for me. I found baby, twenty pounds, sufficient weight. Lizzie Anderson saw me before I got to the house and hurried to welcome me. Harry and Minnie (her children) were delighted with Alvin and wanted to bargain for him right away. I am tired tonight and I am off to bed.

November 18, 1876
Goat Island

Left Lizzie this morning, after promising to return in a few days, and Captain Anderson went with me to Front Street Wharf. We waited fully an hour before the government boat came and then we heard that she, "The Katy" was bound for Alcatraz to convey some soldiers and I had to wait another hour before she returned. Now if ever you found yourself delayed, you can pity me. Everything packed snugly in a satchel and baby just as uncomfortable as a baby can be in three hours neglect, hungry too and his mother wearing a double breasted polonaise. As dinner was out of the question. Well we finally did arrive at the Island and found Captain, Mrs. Francis and Anna waiting for us. We are now enjoying ourselves finely. They had a splendid turkey dinner ready and I did justice to it for my appetite was made sharp by the salt water. This is a very pleasant place to live for the Oakland ferry boats pass the house every half hour. First you see "El Capitan" then "Alameda" and many other boats for different purposes. Spent a very agreeable evening talking to Captain Francis about folks he knew from Half Moon Bay.

November 19, 1876

Sunday on Goat Island was a very quiet day. I came very near getting homesick but tried to be as pleasant as possible. In the afternoon Captain Francis took Anna and myself over the mountain to the other side of the island where we had a close view of the fog whistle and bell also the lighthouse. Captain took us through each of the places and explained every screw, valve etc. I received a very instructive lesson and want to remember all I can of it. In the evening we talked and read. Anna is going to bed and as I sleep with her I will retire also.

November 20, 1876

We all got up early this morning for Anna goes to the Oakland Seminary and had to be present when the School opened so her father took her over to Oakland in his rowboat about seven o'clock this morning. She hated to go and leave the baby but it could not be helped. I washed a number of things for baby, a white wrapper and some bibs. Ate lunch and intended to return to the City on the steamer, but just missed it and Captain Francis rowed his boat to the City Wharf with Alvin and myself. I felt a little timid when in the center of the bay, but the baby laughed all the time at the oars as he splashed the water. No doubt he wanted a bath.

November 21, 1876

Here I am at Lizzie's again. When I got back from the island last night, I left the baby with Lizzie's servant girl and Lizzie and I went to the San Jose Depot to meet Lil. We brought some oranges and had time enough to eat two apiece before the cars came. Lil was glad to find us waiting for her and we took the streetcar and went home in high glee. Took supper, played piano an hour and went to bed. Lil and I lay awake a long time talking.

November 21, 1876
Continued

After breakfast and washing Alvin we got ready to go to the Photograph Gallery to have some pictures taken. I did intend to have baby but he got so fidgety I got provoked. Lil had a dozen Cabinet pictures taken; two positions and I think both are good. After that we went shopping and Lizzie bought stockings. I bought shoes, sound leather ones at that, buttoned clear up the leg and paid five dollars for them. Lil bought several things for Christmas I guess as she would not let me go with her. I bought Harry a candy soldier for his tree and a cradle of babies for Minnie. Lizzie and I bought some fine embroidery. I got enough cross bar linen, for baby two aprons. We did not get back to supper till after six. All are tired, aching feet, ankles beat, must retreat, horrid street.

November 22, 1876

Left Lizzie's this morning, and Lil and I have been walking the streets till we can scarcely move. We ate supper at the California Restaurant and took a room at Wadsworth House on Bush Street for the night. We always go there for it is very convenient and there are some nice folks keeping it and we feel more like home. Lil is now in bed coaxing me to come. Baby is asleep. I must use my new crimping pins and put the gas out.

November 23, 1876

Lil and I got up rather late this morning as we seemed to feel attracted to the bed somehow. We ate breakfast and went out to finish our shopping. Then took the Clay Street rolling car. Went to Taylor Street, got out and called on Mrs. Brown on Pleasant Street. Found Julia, Emma Brown and Jennie Dolloff at home. After spending about an hour, we walked up to Larkin Street to call on Mrs. Sarah Brown, she insisted on us remaining to lunch which we were glad to do and I ate two mutton chops, three potatoes, three slices of bread and drank 3 cups of tea. Honor

Bright, no fibs. I was very hungry and thirsty, besides you know the baby must be fed. " I tinks by and by he will have a toot and can eat for himself." We had a pleasant time. Mrs. Brown gave me a picture of herself.

November 24, 1876

As Lil and I were walking along Montgomery Street who should we overtake but Dr. McGurdy and Cora. I could judge by the style of their dress that they were just married. Doctor had a new suit on and looked as if he had jumped out of a sandbox. Cora wore a white necktie and white kid gloves, a brown traveling dress etc. We accused them on the spot and they acknowledged but bound us to keep the secret a week as they did not wish a serenade. Weather very fine. We are all done with making purchases and start for homeward tomorrow.

November 25, 1876

Met an old friend this morning, Mr. Worn, he was telling us of a sad accident to his sister Mrs. Baugh. She was attempting to light the fire by the aid of coal oil when she set herself on fire and was fearfully burnt. She died a few hours after. We took the 3:20 train for San Mateo and are now safe at the house of Mrs. Price an old friend of Mother's. We had supper and Lil held the baby while I helped wash the dishes, chatting all the while with Mrs. Price. She has just returned from her Centennial trip and brought the chills and fever with her. She is beginning to shake now and I began to laugh ha ha he he he.

November 26, 1876

Got up this morning with a cold in my noodle on account of sleeping with the windows up. The room we slept in had a hot fire and Lil said, "O dear, we will smother, let us get some air." So up went the window and we got cold before morning. Could have gone to church if it had not been for baby and might have heard your favorite minister Mr. Rouse. San Mateo folks seem to be tired of him. At any rate I had the pleasure of hearing the Church bells ring and of seeing others going to the several meetings, some Catholic, some to Mr. Bremers and some to hear Mr. Rouse. Weather is very warm, sunny and bright.

November 27, 1876

Came home on noon stage. We had lots and lots of traps it did seem: baby, satchel, paper bundle, hanging basket for flowers, parasol and two extra shawls. We felt almost ashamed to get off the stage for Mr. Taft, after much coaxing, let me ride outside with baby on account of my getting sick inside. We were very glad to get home for it seemed like rest to us. We had tramped so much, seen so many strange faces, so much gaiety displayed in the windows that we were tired body, eyes and tongues and glad to get home to rest. It makes me think of the beautiful hymn." There is rest for the weary." Comforting words.

November 28, 1876

Came up to the Mill this afternoon. I forgot to say that Ruf came to H.M. Bay to meet me and was so glad to see baby and me. He says it seemed to him like a month that I had been away. It makes me feel glad to find all to make you so welcome home. (as written.) Found everything is apple pie order. Maggie had made a new white apron for Alvin and it fits nicely. Found two letters waiting my return.

November 29, 1876

Washing today and a big pile of dirty clothes too for baby had to have clean skirts and aprons every day while absent from home, but we have a running spring at the door and plenty of soap and considerable elbow grease. Baby is fretty today and seems to have a cold on his lungs. I hope it will not be anything serious for the diphtheria is raging in the City and he may have caught it.

November 30, 1876

Ruf went to H. M. Bay this morning to get something for baby. He is very much choked up and we were unable to sleep last night on account of the rattling in his throat. I put hot onion poultice on his

chest. Ruf got back at four o'clock, found baby
worse, so we took him right down to the Doctor who
prescribed warm bath and Ipecac for an emetic. After
he vomited he was relieved a little.

December 1, 1876

Have concluded to remain down home for a few days as it will be near medical aid: also where Ma can advise me what to do for baby. Gave him an emetic three times today and he raised a large quantity of phlegm. Put a flannel with goose grease on chest and back between shoulders. He is better this evening. Mrs. Davids and Mrs. Doloff have just gone from here. Weather quite cold, we keep a fire in the sitting room all day and eve.

December 2, 1876

Ventured to give baby a bath this morning and continue using Ipecac several times a day. Ruf is quite anxious about the little fellow. He went home to see to things and came right back this evening. Fannie Freitas came over to call on Cora McGurdy but was afraid to come in my room on account of having her baby with her and was cautious for sore throat is catching and I do not blame her.

December 3, 1876

Alvin is much better. He laughed a little at father. They all make such a pet of him that I fear I shall have a spoiled boy to carry home and will have to review my valuable teachings of the past few months. Lil went to Church.

December 4, 1876

Came home to my "lot in the woods" this morning. Baby is six months old today. His cold is almost well. I suppose the change of places, visiting in new air, sleeping in spare rooms that are seldom used did it. I will be almost afraid to take him off again in a hurry. How sad it would be to lose the little darling, just as we are so attached to him, but he is not ours and we ought not wrap our every thought up in him, for we only have him till God sees fit to take him from us. How distant the days we know not. Let us do our duty in caring for the charge in our keeping and if permitted to bring him up to manhood. May he be a good and noble man and may God help us to teach him in a manner that will please him.

December 5, 1876

Have new neighbors over the way in the large brown house owned by the firm, Borden and Hatch. They are a man and wife name Stevens, no children, been married twelve years. We invited them over to supper as they were tired and moving is unpleasant business. I think I shall like the lady very much. She is some years older than I and may have more sense. hm hm.

December 6, 1876

Maggie went home today to make a dress for her sister, Laura and I find I can do my cooking fully as well as to have her here to do it for me. She is not very neat unless I keep a close watch on her every move and as baby is so very good I think I shall tell her I can get along without her in future. I suppose I will find it quite a task at first, but I will give the washing out and think with a little aid from Ruf I can manage to get along this winter. Weather too good. Farmers are calling for rain and the country needs it very much.

December 7, 1876

Father was up to the Mill before breakfast this morning to tell me how sick Ma was and to bring me down home to help take care of her. She has a boil on her back. It is small in size at present but is much inflamed and threatens to be sore. She has a large carbuncle also on her left hip. It is a fearful sight. It occupies a space the size of a hand and is so tender she will scream if you attempt to touch it. The doctor has burnt a number from coming by painting the surface with Iodine, but if they are bound to come I believe the Old Nick could not put them back.

December 8, 1876

Alvin and I slept with Lil last night and she not being used to three in the bed did not rest well so complains of headache today. Ma is not feeling even comfortable today. She has a great deal of pain from her side. Weather quite windy this morning but calm now. Mary Davids spent the evening, Cora and Dr. coaxed me to let them have baby a while in their room so now I hear his voice laughing and expect they are doing all in their power to please him.

December 9, 1876

Father discharged his steward today, so Wesley is waiting on table till another takes his place. Hear that Mr. Taft has a child sick with diphtheria. Mrs. Nichols is to go and help take care of it as the mother is completely worn out watching by the bedside. Ma is a little easier as the carbuncle broke. Ruf went up home but told me to stay till Ma had entirely recovered. So I have a nice little room near Ma and directly under Lil's room (she has changed her room since you were here) so that baby and I have it very snug. Father cannot bear to have him sleep long in the daytime for he wants to play with the little fellow all he can so he sleeps good at night to make up for lost time.

December 10, 1876

How sacred and how innocent
A country life appears
How free from turmoil - discontent
From flattery or fears

Did not go to church this morning but went this evening to S.S. Concert. I took Alvin because I was afraid he would annoy Ma if I left him at home although she insisted upon staying and taking care of him. The concert was very fine. Mr. Todd, the new minister, seemed to take such an interest in the school, so did his wife. She led the singing and in fact all the exercises were arranged by her. She appears like an amiable woman. There was a good deal of singing and moving the organ back-and-forth. Baby stood it pretty well till a large boy got up to speak. He threw his arms and made a great many gestures and baby thought it time to put in a word so he began his da da da da and you should have seen Maria Jane get out of that Church in double quick time.

December 11, 1876

Gave my washing to be done by a Portuguese woman. She is poor and needs help more than the Chinamen about here. Gave baby a bath and will now darn my shawl. I was so smart, I took a new shawl and went to tie baby in the chair and tore a big piece. What do you think of that?

December 12, 1876

Ma has been feeling worse all day and her side is very much inflamed. She has no appetite and I have been trying to coax it by getting a young pigeon and intend to broil it for her supper. She ate a small piece of toast today, that is all. Weather is very fine, not at all like winter.

December 13, 1876

Mr. Taft lost his child, a dear a little girl named Minnie, four years old. She died of diphtheria and was buried today over here in the Odd Fellow's Ground. Mrs. Taft was too ill to attend the funeral. A great many of the friends came over the mountain among them was Mr. and Mrs. Price. They came here to dinner and stayed a while at our house. Ma has been very sick today, so bad that father has decided to go to the city in the morning and consult another physician. Weather bright and pleasant.

December 14, 1876

Father went to the City. Ruf accompanied him. They drove over the mountain in the buggy then took 9:30 train, had a few hours in the City and got back home at seven o'clock. They saw one of San Francisco's best doctors, got medicine and advice and although Ma has not commenced taking it, she seems to feel better already. We keep flax seed poultices[19] and onion on her side and wash it once a day.

December 15, 1876

Mrs. Davids and Mary spent the evening here. Baby says papa or baba and mama now. It sounds real cunning. He tried to sit alone but fell over and bumped his noodle. Ma is getting along nicely. I made her a tapioca pudding and she relished it. Weather like summer.

December 16, 1876

Ruf went up to the Mill today to attend to his horses. He says he feels real lonesome up there without me and I suppose he means it but still he does not want me to go home till Ma has entirely recovered. Two ladies called, one was speaking of a young girl she met at the store, the other lady (who was almost a stranger to her) asked a description of the person. "Well she wore a high hat with black feather, a brown dress and was a remarkable homely girl. She seemed to be flirting with the store keeper. Do you know who she is?" It was my eldest sister replied the lady. Oh dear how bad I felt for them both. Just think what an awkward stillness fell on the entire room. I wanted to get out and guess the others would have gone through a small sized rat hole if one has been in sight. Received

---

[19] Flaxseed poultice can be used for burns, ulcerated wounds, insect bites, boils and skin infections.

a nice long letter from Lotte Searls at Washington. It had a present in it for a baby and came through in eight days.

December 17, 1876

Ma was feeling pretty well so I went to Church with Lil this evening. A lady came to stay with Ma and told me to leave baby and not feel uneasy for if he awoke she would take care of him. The sermon was from St. John, "If the Son shall make you free ye shall be free indeed." He touched upon several very interesting sketches about freedom. He spoke of a sale of slaves and said at the sale was an old colored preacher who had been saving up his money to try and buy his freedom. Bidders began to put up twenty, thirty, forty, sixty dollars. The poor negro's heart sank when he heard one man bid seventy. Then all was still, finding no opposition the poor fellow arose and bid seventy five and thus was able to buy himself. I felt so glad, it seem to me I had witnessed the whole affair myself. Mr. Todd pictured it so complete. Got home, found all right and must poultice Ma and hasten to bed.

December 18, 1876

Got up at eight o'clock, washed baby and after lying in bed took a nice long ride with Ma. She had to be pillowed in the buggy but by driving slow the air did her good. We went as far as Amesport and returned in time for dinner. The salt air gave her an appetite, but I won't say anything about my own. It is generally too good.

December 19, 1876

Took another nice ride. I drove Fannie but she knows the difference in my handling and did not want to go well at all. Ma took the lines for a minute and she picked up her ears and trotted off. We took baby today for we started after his morning nap and the little minx saw us get our hats on and he crowed to go. Ma held him on her lap. He is quite heavy. Roads rather dusty.

December 20, 1876

Ruf came down this evening. Says things are all right in the Redwoods. Lil went out for a while this afternoon. I go with Ma to ride because I will not be down here when she is well and then when I am gone Lil will have plenty of chances to go. We took baby again and he sat very quiet till he saw the horse switch her tail, then he wanted to grab it and kept up a movement all the way home.

December 21, 1876

Too good a time to last long. Took a delightful drive to a place down a long lane where the vegetable man lives. We saw some lovely gardens and many fine gum trees. Ma gave me a lesson in cooking. Told me how to make a beefsteak pie with mashed potatoes over it nicely browned. Also how to make a mince pie. If I keep her instructions in mind, I will have some genuine cooking when I get home.

December 22, 1876

Father engaged a good cook to come and make the cakes as he is to have the supper here for the ball on Christmas night. So I have been giving the orders about cakes: plain, raisin, currant, jelly and other kinds, frosted and ornamental fancy. The costumer has arrived with two large chests full of costumes as it is to be a grand Masquerade given by H.M.B. Cornet Band.

December 23, 1876

Very busy day for most everyone. Ma went downstairs to supervise the pie business and give a few other orders but she gets weak quick. Her knees are not very strong yet. Lil has been preparing the apples for the tables. I have done but little as some of my time is devoted to baby and some to watching Ma for fear she will not be prudent in taking care of herself.

December 24, 1876

Ruf is here and I expect we will have a pleasant Christmas. Did not go to Church for there was a great deal to be seen to and Lil could not leave home to go with me. I am now going to bed early for tomorrow will be a busy day and I have yet my hair to frizz and my long legged stocking to hang up. Dr. McCurdy hung the baby's sock up and filled it with candy and nuts. Lil and Ruf went to the Christmas tree at the Church. Brought a hood for Alvin, Ma sent it.

December 25, 1876

Father wished me a Merry Christmas about two o'clock this morning, and I felt so sleepy that I could not realize it was Christmas. The bells had been ringing and the Catholic Band had been playing and a great many people had been to mass, but I slept through it all. I got up at daylight and looked at my presents. I forgot to mention that as Ma's presents were too large to put in the stockings, we tied the bottoms of her unmentionables and put the things in them. You should have seen how funny they looked. My presents were: "Sights and Insights" by Mrs. Whitney, from Ma. A beautiful blue and gold autograph album from Lil. A set of mats worked on Java canvas with blue and salmon colored worsted from Jennie Dolloff and a large album for photographs from Ruf. It holds 24 Cabinet pictures and 80 common sized photographs. The binding is dark red leather with very strong clasp. I think I was pretty well booked this year don't you?

I must now go and assist them with setting the tables for the Ball supper as we expect quite a crowd and will have to sit up till about two o'clock as the first tables will be filled at twelve and it takes them some time to eat. I will try and write our particulars tomorrow night.

December 26, 1876

Well, we are all sleepy tonight and have been blinking our eyes all day, but I guess I can pry them open long enough to give you a few items. We had everything in readiness about ten o'clock and then sat down to rest. We were cheated from looking into Pacific Hall for the managers had put thick white curtains up. At twelve they began to march in and Ruf was door-keeper. I stood in the hall and saw them pass. Such ridiculous images. Some as shepherds, Indian, Negro and in fact everything. Women in domino[20] of every color and in fancy rigs of every description. Some were very laughable characters. About seventy five ate supper. We got up at ten o'clock and ate some cold chicken etc. Ma busied herself in putting her storeroom to rights and cleaning up in general. I put on a suit of a shepherdess and Cora tried the Highland Lass. We did not let any but our family see us though. I had a blue cambric mask and she had a white one. Well I guess I shall retire. And as my name is Ria, will sit beside the fire and write to a

---

[20] Domino: a long, loose cloak usually worn with a half mask as a masquerade costume.

big . . . I wish you a very Merry Christmas my Dear.

December 27, 1876

Feel more like myself today. I slept so sound last night that Ma came into my room in the night and I did not hear her. She says I was lying on the very edge of the bed and in a moment more would have tumbled out. Then what a smash there would have been! Alvin weighs twenty pounds. Don't you think that quite a lump of a boy? Ruf went to Redwood City this morning to attend to a mortgage he has on a house over here. I wanted to go with him thinking I would then have a few hours with Clara Shelly, but he was afraid we could not return till late and baby might get cold.

December 28, 1876

The weather still continues fine. Ma and I took a ride toward Purissima but the road being rough in that direction, we did not enjoy our ride much. We went humpy, bumpy, chunky and then Ma would say "O my side," so we came back and drove a short ways on the toll road.

December 29, 1876

The year is drawing to its close and it makes me feel real lonely on account of parting with my companion in thought namely this journal of my daily doings. It sets me to wondering: first, if it will ever prove a benefit my noting down these common place events of everyday life, and second, if Clara will think it worthwhile to waste her noble mind reading my trash.

December 30, 1876

Saturday and the last working day in this year. Ruf says I may stay down here till after New Year's day so I am rejoiced, I assure you, for when I do choose to go back to my redwood cottage I know Ma will be feeling well and I am satisfied to live there when I know all are well at home. I spent a few minutes in Mrs. McCurdy's room chatting with her and the Doctor. He is just as jolly as ever and we passed many a jest.

December 31, 1876

Now I have been preparing your mind several times for the last day in the year. Well, it has arrived and I intended to make a big speech: a great pow-wow but like the schoolboy (up to make a speech) my words fail me and I can't say much. This is the Sabbath and I am going to Church in a few moments to hear the last sermon of the year. As I have no chance to send my book over to Clara, I will write for the month of January for paper is still plentiful and if I tried I might manage to stretch the whole next year's account in the same book.

Maria and Edna

Rufus Harvey Hatch, courtesy
San Mateo County Historical Association Collection
(1964.107.15.).

Alvin, Rufus, Edna, Clara
Family portrait many years after Maria's death.

Alvin Hatch circa 1900. Courtesy San Mateo County Historical
Association Collection (1964.107.15.).

Clara Hatch Kneese

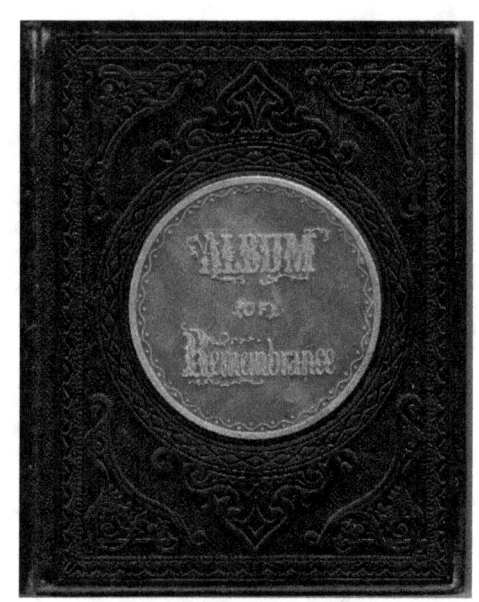

Maria's Album of Remembrance.

Edna having fun in the waves.

Rufus Hatch

Rufus in his later years.

Virginia Lodge, a summer home built by Edna and her husband,
Dr. J. C. McGovern in Purissima Canyon around 1910.

Clara's Album of Remembrance

1877

January 1, 1877

I wish you a Happy New Year

Mr. Taft buried his little baby today. What a sad greeting to a new year.

January 2, 1877

Ruf went to Redwood again today. We had turkey dinner and it did taste real good. I wish you could have had a bite but if you had been here you might have taken more than your share and poor me would have had to suffer. I must pick up my traps[21] and travel home tomorrow. Ma is much better and I am able to leave. I have been down here most a month and it is high time for me to travel.

January 3, 1877

Ruf brought Clara's Journal back with him and I am so anxious to read it but have allowed myself to read but a few pages in it as I had to come up home

---

[21] Traps: personal belongings; luggage.

to the woods today. Found everything in order for I have such a good husband. He made new sills to all the doors and planed the work table for me. I was awful lonesome all afternoon and guess it would make one of your 'blue' days.

January 4, 1877

Baby is seven months old today and he sits alone on the floor for hours and plays with an old yeast-powder can filled with coffee beans and a clothes pin for a doll. He is not a particle of trouble but it is a real blessing. He is lazy about getting teeth as he has only the print of them under the skin. Been cooking most all day, made two cream cakes and a jelly cake, besides chicken pot pie.

January 5, 1877

Made mince meat today. Ruf chopped the meat, suet and apples for me and picked the raisins. When I was ready to put the raisins in, I found but half the quantity that I had laid out. He says he don't know where they went but I guess if I could dissect his stomach I would roost on a raisin mound. I put up a jar of mince meat and made one pie (the first mince pie I ever made) and it is de-lic-ious, no joking.

January 6, 1877

Well I have been reading the month of Jan 76 in your Journal. It is just splendid and seems like you are sitting here with arms folded telling me what you had been about at home and I read so steady I could hardly see the words when I closed the book. Now I will read for Feb next time I have a moment all by myself for when Ruf is here in the quiet hours he wants to read aloud to me and it always happens to be about the "Legislature" or men's affairs of some kind and I have to listen and pretend I am wonderfully interested. All the time I am thinking of something else and hoping he will stop reading aloud. And when he does end I give a sigh of relief and say, "Goodness, who would have thought it," as if I had heard every word.

January 7, 1877

This is Sunday and I am up in my cottage house. It always seems so lonely here on Sunday because the men are not at work and I miss the "Gee," "Haw," "Whoa bony," "Back Pete," to the oxen hauling logs. So I have employed my time this afternoon in reviewing old letters. I have my top bureau drawer full of old letters and a big pile of them are from you. I have also a great many poems written by Violetta (whoever she is) and here is one I think so pretty.

Pure Gems

If angels should covet a gem from the earth
I would be no bright bauble we hold of great worth;
But could tears of repentance be crystallized, then
An angel might wish to possess one of them.
And many dear saints, when their labors are done,
May find when their crowns of rejoicing are won—
The gems in each crown which most brilliantly glow
Be the penitent tears which they have caused to
flow.

January 8, 1877

Did a little washing this morning some baby aprons, (and what you call um's) and ironed this afternoon. Ruf went down to Purissima on horseback and I wrote two letters so that he could mail them. I have been putting the photographs in my large Album and have it full. One hundred pictures, beside a good many framed on the wall.

January 9, 1877

I have been cleaning my parlor today. The tidy of spatter work made by Cousin Mary looks very pretty on my centre table. Read a while in Clara's book and counted the number of times she went to see Mrs. Snow in a month. Found she "run over" twenty times one month. Thank my lucky stars I am not her neighbor. How I should be bothered with her interrupting my work and putting her clack in at every chance. Poor Mrs. Snow, I know how to pity her.

January 10, 1877

My new neighbor Mrs. Stevens came over to lunch today. She is a very pleasant lady, has no children, has been married eleven years and is at present making "chicken fixings." So I have to ransack my drawers, (not my unmentionables) to find a small pattern for her. We had sardines, preserved cherries, bread and butter for lunch, no cake. If I had caught sight of her coming, I would have rolled up my sleeves and daubed a little flower on my nose pretending I was baking, but alas!

January 11, 1877

Ruf brought some pumpkin from the saw mill and I went into pie business in earnest. Ma told me to take one pound of flour to 1/2 lb. of lard and butter, so I weighed about six lbs. of flour and goodness me I have crust enough to make forty pies but I only had pumpkin for one, so I just made the crust as thick as I could so as not to have as much left over. (One fib)

January 12, 1877

Ruf has gone to bed and the fire is going out so I am awful lonesome and wish I could see you and let my tongue loose instead of scribbling to you. I guess you will get tired of this home writing and will not find it very interesting. In looking my last few days account over, I see that I have neglected the weather report but it has been about as usual. That is very pleasant and too good for farmers. We need rain so badly.

January 13, 1877

Came down to father's this afternoon. Will stay overnight. Ruf has gone to the Lodge, Father is playing with baby, Ma is reading a sermon in the "Evangel" and Lily is mending her stockings. I had a very cold ride down from the Mill. Many children have whooping cough around here and I will have to be careful of Alvin.

Good night,
Blow out the light,
And snore all you might,
You have the right,
When you are tight.

January 14, 1877

O how frightened we all have been. I can scarcely tell you about it. At twelve o'clock in the night Ma was awakened with a cry of fire. She gave the alarm and in a few moments all the inmates of the Hotel were up and dressed. The fire was on the opposite side of the street and looked so near to us that we gathered up our clothing, jewelry and choice things and tied them in blankets ready to throw out. Our men folks went to help put out the fire if possible. They worked till five in the morning and got the fire down before it reached the store. Although the building caught fire a number of times and the men had taken out most of the goods, the saloon and restaurant were burnt to the ground and a small house that stood between the store and restaurant. Ruf holds a mortgage on the place that was burnt and it is insured for one thousand only, so he will lose some by the fire too. We feel so bad today after the fright that we hardly say anything but "fire." the men of the town all turned out and some rang the church bells and school bell while others threw on water. You see, if the Hotel had caught, of course it would throw sparks so far being a tall building that the whole town would soon have been in flames. O, how we all prayed for a hard rain, but everything was so dry, we feel half sick all of us.

January 15, 1877

More about the fire. They find out it was set on fire by some thieves who wished to plunder. For in several other places in the same street coal oil has been spread to make it burn. In the brewery and blacksmith shop and a good many things were stolen from the store. Two dozen new axes, two dozen water pails and any quantity of pants, coats and woolen shirts. For while men were trying to put the fire out others were stealing!

January 16, 1877

Ruf went to Redwood to see Mr. Fox about his mortgage. He met Mr. Shelly but being on business and having but a few moments to spare, he could not go to see Clara although kindly invited to take lunch with her. If I had been in her place I would be glad that he did not trouble me to get lunch for him as long as he left Maria at home. I heard one laughable thing about the fire. When the men could not get pails to carry water they ran to the store and grabbed the new "domestic utensils" and one would say, "Pass the bowl." Another, "Hand us a jug" and a third, "Hurry up with that pee pot." It must have been amusing anyhow for there was a group of women who heard it.

January 17, 1877

It began to sprinkle this morning just as we were preparing to go up to the Mill so we thought we would wait till after dinner and then it started to rain in good earnest. So here we are for tonight. Cora and Dr. are spending the evening with us. They brought two new games with them of picture cards. One is "Old Maid" the other is "One, Two, Three." Both are laughable and we expect a pleasant evening. We are now waiting for Ruf to come up and join us as it needs one more hand to make it interesting. It is beginning to hail and Cora says she will make some ice cream for us. Wish you could step in.

January 18, 1877

Came up home today. Got soaked with rain as it began soon after we got halfway here so when we reached home I took baby and went to my neighbors as she had a good fire. Ruf started two fires in our house and when I got dry, I came over and did not take cold. I guess I kept "Cub" well wrapped up. It seems awful quiet here after being down home. I get real homesick especially just after being away a few days. It rains hard at present, good for everybody. It makes the farmers as smiling as a basket of chips.

January 19, 1877

Been cooking all day for we had nothing in the house to eat. I brought up some yeast and intend to have buckwheat cakes for breakfast tomorrow. I do not make bread. My neighbor has no chickens and we have plenty and lots of eggs so we trade (that is, we women do). I give her one half dozen eggs for a small loaf of bread, and we eat very little bread so I do not have to bother with it.

January 20, 1877

O dear, just think how old I am getting. This is my birthday and the second one recorded in this book, twenty seven. Only think of it, my! It makes my head itch. I am trying to catch you and will soon be able to. Don't you go so fast, but stop. Lil is ahead of us both. Ma gave me a handsome moss album and Lil gave me her choice mosses to fill it. Wasn't that a nice present?

January 21, 1877

Ruf had to go to Purissima for the mail today, so I hurried and scribbled a few lines to Ma. She will be pleased to get it. Read a letter from San Francisco and one from Miss Hauss in San Mateo. Baby has been lots of company for me today for the roads being slippery Ruf had to ride slow and did not get home till teatime. I suppose you were at Church as usual and now while I think of it, let me give you a word of "chirking." I see many times dear friend that you have the "blues." You have no business with such things for you have your home in a pleasant place and your Church (your best friend) ever near. Here I am deprived of going but very seldom, and living in the woods with but one strange neighbor and yet I am never "blue" fact I sometimes get lonely but I won't allow myself to keep it long, I just work as hard as I can or sing or walk in the road a ways. Don't think I am scolding you it is only a gentle reproof. I know I do not suffer as you do and there you may have a small excuse but don't get blue over it if you can help it.

January 22, 1877

Washed a few things and baked some biscuits and a gold cake with yolks of eight eggs. It ought to be gold I think. Here is the recipe of a cake I make and it is splendid.

Feather cake
1 cup sugar
1 cup milk
2 1/2 cups flour
1 tablespoon butter
one large egg
1 1/2 teaspoons yeast powder
essence lemon or cinnamon

January 23, 1877

Baby had the colic today and has taken up some of my time. I arranged my mosses and ferns in my new Album and played a piece on the piano "Beatrice di Tendi" from Italian opera. Picked a bouquet besides my sweeping and dusting. Weather very fine.

January 24, 1877

Father brought Lil up here this morning and said she could stay a few days with me. Father had to go right back so as to get there stage time. I was busy making cream cake when they came and I was so glad to see them I hardly knew whether I stood on my head or heels for a while. This is the first time Lil has been up here this winter and it seems so nice to have her. We have done nothing much but talk this afternoon.

January 25, 1877

Lil helped me with my morning work and then

went in search of ferns. She came back half crazy over some gold backs she had found. I suppose you know them, they are the sweetest of all ferns I think. Ruf calls them "gray backs." We had lunch and have been busy all afternoon pressing ferns. We have the large books full and smoothing irons are in demand for weight. We are now going to have some popcorn and apples. Lil says I am a good cook. I keep making her eat all the time, good chance to get rid of my poor scraps when I have company. Don't you want to come?

January 26, 1877

Lil, Alvin and I have just got home. We went to spend the afternoon and take tea with our neighbor as Ruf went to Spanishtown to the Free Mason's Lodge and started from here at two o'clock and will not be home till twelve tonight, but it is a lovely moonlight and will be a pleasant ride though lonely. Lil and I intend to sit up and wait for him. We are to sew on two white aprons for baby. Ruf promised to bring some candy and I want a bite of it before I go to bed. We had some floating islands[22] for supper and I have felt sort of floaty ever since. Well, good night.

January 27, 1877

Ruf says Lil will have to go home tomorrow as Ma is not very strong and has been doing Lil's work

---

[22] Floating Islands: a dessert consisting of meringue floating on a vanilla custard.

besides her own and is not able to do it long. Lil has been out most all day gathering ferns so as to have a variety and some green tree moss for a hanging basket. She gave me some ferns and I give you some of them in this book. The sea mosses are some I floated and the leaves are some I pressed last year. They are not very pretty but would look better if varnished. Mrs. Stevens came over a while this evening and we had singing and playing. She is real pleasant company and I enjoy her visits very much. Lil is now packing her valise for her departure tomorrow.

January 28, 1877

Lil went home today and I miss her very much. It looked so much like rain. I did not venture out so have been alone all day. It rained real hard about three o'clock but Ruf just escaped it. He brought me in a very "chirky" letter from Clara. Eight pages, just the kind of letter I like to get, a good long one, but hers contained some very sad news. The death of Miss Goodwin a schoolteacher. I had never met her but have heard her spoken of many times and know she must have been a good, kind young woman. Ruf got a letter from Geo Fox so we were both very quiet for a few moments feasting on the contents.

January 29, 1877

Has been raining very hard all day and it made

the stoop so wet that your dear Myra came right down on her seat of honor in front of my very door. Just think of it. It makes my back bone creak to write it, but I hopped up and took a long breath. Hereafter will walk as if eggs were under foot when I go out. I am going to bed early tonight for I love to hear the rain on the roof, it makes me think of the song.

> What a joy to press the pillow,
> Of a cottage chamber bed,
> And to listen to the patter,
> Of the soft rain overhead.
> Let us snore.

January 30, 1877

Rain all day long. Ruf has been in the house all the afternoon till time to feed his horses. I don't think he enjoys being in the house for I always rake my brain over to find something to set him to work at. First, "Ruf, please fill the small coal oil can." Then, "Ruf, will you fill my molasses pitcher, the keg is so heavy." And finally, "Ruf, the baby wants to go to you awful bad, just take the little fellow, he is tired of sitting on the floor." So I guess he doesn't read much and dislikes these rainy days.

January 31, 1877

At last. O, dear! I hate to say farewell dear journal, and even as I write a stray tear is found in each eye for it seems like a living person I have been addressing each night instead of a book. I know the best of friends must part and I cast my eye on a small book just half your size that contains a mine of worth to me and it had to be parted with and I dare say a sigh of regret was its' finishing touch. Regret that the year was so short, and the book is well filled and in relation is Corsican to you. In looking the pages over I find that I have had to note down several deaths in our neighborhood and feel thankful that during the past year both Clara and I have been permitted to live to finish our journals. How sad it would have been had one of us been taken and our book left unfinished. I also find that in the last year I have become a Mother and Clara has raised to a step higher, that of Aunt Clara. I have also passed two birthdays and I'm getting older and not handsomer every day. All these things make me value the book and am glad to have a dear friend who will excuse all mistakes and who will pardon all sayings that she may think improper at the same time remembering I am no worse than I appear to be, and I compliment myself in looking it over to find I have told but few fibs!

January 31, 1877

To Clara
To you dear friend this book I give,
Tis filled with records past,
May you and I as years we live,
Be loving to the last.

When on this book your eyes you bend,
Pray think of me, your hearts true friend,
And though far distant I may be,
O, look at this and think of me.
Myra

When this you read,
You'll say I need,
To bag my head,
And run to bed.
No poetess of great renown,
Could read these lines without a frown.

M.

The End

1878

January 1, 1878

Dear Journal,

After nearly a year has passed I again take you in my hand intending to use you as before for the purpose of writing down things important, and not important, sensible and not sensible, sad and gay, bright or gloomy, but all of them to concern or be of interest to the one for whom it is intended should be sole reader and for the writer herself in after years. So I will proceed to business. In the first place I begin this year in the same manner I did 1876, namely sleepy. I went to a party New Year's Eve and did not get home till six o'clock in the morning. Ruf and Lil went also and I left Alvin with Ma. I have not had any chance to sleep so I am a very stupid person today. Father and Ma invited us there to turkey dinner and I shall have to begin to rub my eyes open. Not to be bright. O no, but in order to see the turkey.

January 2, 1878

Feel better after a good rest and sound sleep last night. I heard that several gentleman called on me yesterday, but I was not at home and was rather glad it happened so for I had not prepared for callers and should have felt annoyed at not treating them.

The weather is very cold now especially in the morning. I go about all doubled over to get warm. Now, although Christmas has passed, I intend to tell you what my presents were; a clock from Ruf, a Russia leather purse and a wire hanging basket from Ma and Father, a book, "True as Steel" by Marion Harland from Lil and a card case of spatter work, a wall basket made of splints from Mrs. Stevens and a match safe and card case in silver card board and red worsted from Lizzie Anderson. Now I think I did very well, I gave Ruf a bird and cage, two pairs of socks and a rustic bottle of cologne. Alvin got a little chair, a music box, a pair of red mittens, a gold ring, a gold dollar and new scarf. I need not say the chair pleased him the most. I think though if his Aunt Clara had sent a spoon holder full of spoons, he would have thanked her by saying "Plea."

January 3, 1878

Made apple and peach pies this morning and ironed a dozen starched pieces, so I took the afternoon for calling. I went to see Ma first, she was not feeling well. I next called on Mrs. Nelson, she was not at home. Then to see Fannie Freitas, she was out. Then to see Mrs. Simmons, she was out so I came home in disgust. I suppose these ladies were doing the same business that I was for one said to me this evening, "I called here today and you were out." "Yes" said I. I called on you today and you were out. She said we were at outs with each other.

January 4, 1878

It is evening and we have a nice fire in the sitting room grate and the room looks real cozy. Ruf and I have our lap full of hickory nuts and apples which we intend to put out of our sight as soon as I finish my scribble. Alvin is playing with his blocks, he is 19 months old today and as cunning as ever. Now he is lugging that doll after him, the one you made and the foot ties cracked open and bran is spilling on the floor. You ought to get out a patent on that doll.

January 5, 1878

How provoking it is to send for the Weekly Post to see the answer to the puzzles and they sent the wrong one. It is a week past, so now I have to live in suspense, till I send for the right one. I do not have much faith in either of us getting a prize, but there is fun in trying for it. Ma is suffering with another boil on her right hip. Ruf has to go to the Odd Fellows Lodge tonight so I will spend the evening at home with my folks though I dread coming home here with baby in the cold.

January 6, 1878

Another Sabbath has begun or ended which do you call it at four in the afternoon? I did not go to Church today. Ruf had to go to the Mill with a man and I could not go in peace with Alvin. He is sure to make a speech so I stayed at home and read and wrote all day. The birds are singing as hard as they can and they are company for me.

January 7, 1878

It has rained hard all day and our trees look green and pretty. The grass is springing and everything looks bright. Arthur Merrill spent the evening with us. He was on his way to Pigeon Point in a schooner, but got so seasick he was obliged to land at Amesport and walk here.

He will stay with Father a couple of days and then walk down to Pescadero. He intends to work in a lumber mill. Ma is feeling better today.

January 8, 1878

This has been quite a pleasant day. I cleaned house. By that I mean took all the chairs etc. out of the rooms and gave the carpets a thorough sweeping, scrubbed the pieces of oilcloth and kept busy all morning. Spent the afternoon with Fannie Freitas. Clarence and Alvin kept up a continual quarrel all the time. Clarence being stronger, knocked Alvin down three or four times. I came home 4 o'clock and got supper. Beef steak, mashed potatoes, canned corn, tea, cookies and cornstarch cream.

January 9, 1878

Let me see what happened today. Received a letter from Clara Shelley and one from Mrs. Todd who is at present at Elk Grove. I wrote two letters to New York, hemmed three towels and one tablecloth, marked them with indelible ink and put new bands on three of Alvin's skirts. Lil send me a dozen nice autumn leaves, varnished.

January 10, 1878

Beautiful weather we are having. It seems almost too fine to stay in the house. Alvin has been out in the garden all morning playing with a little pail of stones and dirt. I received a box from Clara containing some tidies, some lace for pillowcases and four yards of beautiful tatting, the sweetest I ever saw for Auntie's sweet Alvin.

January 11, 1878

Lillie Noyes came today to stay for a few days with me. She says it seems like home here. She took Alvin for a walk in the afternoon as far as the beach. I got a package from San Mateo today. Mrs. Price sent some things over that I had left at her house. I forgot my hair crimpers among other things but she said I need not care if my hair is not crimped as long as I am married. You and I do not think so do we? Wrote a letter to Lizzie also one to Bell and Co.

January 12, 1878

Received another large letter from Cousin Robert. He had to pay nine cents to send it and it is the most comical letter you ever saw. Full of engravings and speeches to match. I wish I had your head here to help me plan an answer to beat his wit. It will be impossible for me to do it without a better head than I have now. Father, Ma and Lil were here to supper. I'll tell you what I had as long as I cooked it—alone. Roast chicken, broiled steak, mashed potatoes, turnips, canned corn, grated horseradish, pickled grapes, bread, tea, preserved pears, crullers and pumpkin pie for dessert. Can you taste any of this? I guess you can smell the pears for they have slices of lemon in them and I know you like the flavor. Ruf went to the Lodge, so did father. Fannie Freitas came to spend the evening so we had a pleasant talk altogether.

January 13, 1878

Sunday and rain. I do believe I like to see rain any day rather than Sunday. It seems so lonely. I am not like the man who prayed, O Lord, let it rain Sundays and nights so the poor laboring man rest. Lil went to church and called for me but Alvin was asleep and Lillie Noyes was preparing to go home and I could not go. Lil got caught in the rain coming from Church. Both of my birds woke Ruf in the night. They were singing by moonlight, I had left the curtains up.

January 14, 1878

Father and Ma were here to lunch today. I sent for them and I'll tell you what we had for lunch, cold sliced tongue, pickled peaches, egg omelet, fried apples in slices, a cup of tea and sponge cake pudding. It resembles the "What is it, pudding?" Ma insisted upon Ruf and myself going back with her at two o'clock. So Alvin and I went and Ruf promised to be there to supper after doing his chores. We had a pleasant day together and came home at eight o'clock. The wind was blowing so hard I could scarcely keep my feet on the ground. Ruf always carries Alvin so I have only myself to look after.

January 15, 1878

Heard that Ellen Johnston is married to Rev Chilson, the young minister who has preached in this place several times. He is some years younger than Ellen, she is 27 and I think she will make a good wife for a minister and she is a good girl and always took part in Sunday school etc. and is a member of Methodist Church.

January 16, 1878

It rained a perfect storm all day and the wind has been blowing so hard I fear the trees will blow down, as several of our huge ones were leaning over a good deal. The roof has blown off of one of the largest houses near town, and flag staffs are bending over. It is a terrible hurricane.

January 17, 1878

It still continues to pour in torrents. Ruf and I were awake nearly all night as we had our heads right by the window and the wind and rain together makes such a racket it was frightful to hear. The water is running in the house in puddles. One reason is the south side of the house needs painting very badly and it lets the water in and another reason is the wind would beat the rain into any place in such weather.

January 18, 1878

The rain ceased in the night, so today has been quite fair. Father came up this morning and says the rooms nearly all leaked in the Hotel. Fanny was in for a few minutes this afternoon but I had no time to go out for my house looked like distress this morning and needed some straightening. Besides, the kitchen stove has smoked so the last few days that I could not cook much but ham or beefsteak, potatoes with boiled eggs for a change. I made some lace for Ma during the wet days.

January 19, 1878

Read about the trouble in San Francisco on

account of a riot or the preparation for a riot; the working men, or Chinamen will have to give up I fear, one or the other will suffer. Went down and spent the afternoon with Ma. Ruf went to the Lodge this eve.

January 20, 1878

I'm so glad my birthday came on Sunday this year. Ma gave me a book, "The Girls," by Mrs. Whitney. Father gave a nice earthen dish for baked beans and Lil gave a handsome scarf, red and silver with crimped fringe. Ruf did not give me anything because he forgot when my birthday came. I went to Church this morning and took Alvin. He was as good and cunning as could be. He sat perfectly still and only spoke once. That was to say "Plea." The minister had a glass of water and took a drink. It was communion Sunday the sermon was preached from "This drink in remembrance of me." Lil came up after Church and stayed all afternoon and evening.

January 21, 1878

Rather gloomy weather today so I mended Ruf's old pants and wish you could enjoy the same blessing, patches and buttons. Fannie came up this evening. Lizzie Nelson and Alice Wolfe spent the afternoon here and we had a pleasant chat.

January 22, 1878

It has been raining and blowing all day and just as dreary as possible. I wrote four letters this morning. The rain made the stove smoke so we could not keep fire there and had rather a slim meal but Ma sent some good soup and that filled vacant places.

January 23, 1878

Weather pleasant. Read a letter from Brother William. The family are all well. He is busy farming in Lompoc. Mr. Chas Elkins one of our neighbors died this morning after an illness of two years, lingering consumption. He leaves a wife and four children. Ruf has gone to a meeting of Sisters of Rebecah. (I think that is spelled wrong.) They have just organized the Order here. I may join after a while.

January 24, 1878

Nothing new today except rain and mud everywhere. Mrs. Levi ran in this morning on her way to the store. She says farmers have enough rain to last them for a month. Got a letter from Miss Hauss and one from Lizzie Anderson. Miss H intended to pay us a visit but writes that her vacation was too short and she will try to come over in the summer.

January 25, 1878

Attended the funeral of Mr. Elkins this afternoon. Mr. Gaffney preached a very feeling sermon for the occasion. He said it was through the influence of a lady (who visited Mr. Elkins) that he became a Christian. He asked for prayer meetings to be held at his house. His wife is a strict Catholic but after trying in vain to persuade him to see the Priest, she gave in and seemed to be contented to have him buried by the Protestants. The sun shone on the grave which made it much better than to have a shower.

January 26, 1878

Made an apple and a cranberry pie this morning. Finished up my regular Saturday work so as to go down to Ma's but just as I got ready to start the rain came down at a 240 gait so I had to content myself with my crochet all the afternoon and nearly died with lonesomeness. Ruf was in reading the paper all the evening so I forgot how lonely I had been.

January 27, 1878

Could not go to Church for it rained hard all day. So I read and wrote part of the time and after dinner sat and looked out the window with Alvin. Ruf brought some nice oranges for me. They did not have preaching in the evening.

January 28, 1878

Not raining today. Mrs. Levie called this morning before my dishes were washed. I don't see how people can spare time to visit so early, I can't and I have but one child while this lady has four who always accompany her to my great (delight.) One got at the keg of white paint and splashed the side of the house outside, another pulled up two young trees that were Ruf's favorites, the third kept bawling for cake every minute and the fourth, thank goodness, was too young to do much but sleep. When Ruf came home and they had gone he was in a bad humor about his paint and trees. They are a match for the celebrated family we met at Mrs. Stevens. (Annoyance)

January 29, 1878

Pleasant weather. Ruf took care of Alvin a couple of hours this afternoon and let me go out to get some calico and to see about getting a common hat for everyday. I ran in to see Ma and Lil. All are well. Ma has been making what she calls a "Cottage by the Sea." She made the cottage of pasteboard and stuck pebbles on which makes it pretty. She has a walk made of pebbles and on one side there is a fernery, on the other side a rockery. It is very fine and well worth $10 dollars. I found all right when I got back. Alvin had told Ruf, "Ugh, ugh" and Ruf was awful glad I happened to come just in time.

January 30, 1878

Wrote a letter to Cousin Robert also one to Mrs. Todd. Received a package from Lizzie Anderson containing a roll of patches and two sweet little aprons - short sleeve, low neck. One has a cording of turkey red in the seams and all around the apron. The other has narrow linen lace on it. Both are very neat. I made an apron like this blue for Alvin today. It is a real good piece and washes well three yards for 25 cts.

January 31, 1878

Ruf has been downtown to see about the Railroad that is to go through here and has just got back.

February 1, 1878

Not much doing today. Ruf and I spend the evening with Mr. and Mrs. Nelson. While there, four others came in and we had a very pleasant time. We were treated to oranges, nuts and candies and came home at ten o'clock. Alvin was as bright as a dollar all the time. We intend to go somewhere every evening till we get our visits paid. No rain but dark nights so we had to carry a lantern.

February 2, 1878

Made cake and pie this morning besides my other duties. Crocheted in afternoon. Mrs. Simmons and two children were here awhile. I had roast pork, mashed potatoes and hot slaw for supper. Here is my recipe, splendid if made right.

Hot Slaw
Quarter or more of tender cabbage chopped pretty fine and put in a dish till other ingredients are ready.
1 teaspoonful mustard
1 teaspoon salt
2 tablespoons cream

1 tablespoon butter
1 cup vinegar
yolks of two eggs beaten
Put it all together (except cabbage) on the fire. Stir constantly. When just to a boil pour on cabbage and cover up till eaten so as to let it steam. It looks like a good deal of trouble but is very easy to do.

Spent evening with Stilson family, came home nine o'clock.

February 3, 1878

Went to church this morning. Sermon 2 Cor, 1 chapter, 6 verse. Alvin was good and went to sleep. Lil came home with me and spent afternoon and evening. Would have gone to evening service but as we were out with Alvin rather late the two evenings before, we thought it best to put him to bed early and go other Sunday evenings. The weather was beautiful all day, just like summer.

February 4, 1878

I declare if it did not have to rain again. It commenced in the night and has kept up all of today. We were greeted with a smoky stove of course. When it rains I always pitch right into the sewing and I darned everything I could find; socks, stockings, dresses etc. and when Ruf came home and I told him about it he said he had been darning some too! But his was about Ames and the squirrel law.

February 5, 1878

Ma sent a nice dish of crullers to me this morning. They came at the right time for we were just out of cake and the hens are having holidays I guess for we got no eggs for two days. The sun has been out all day and "chirked" us up a good deal. I went over and got Wesley's three children and they played here till noon and made all the noise they could. Alvin joined in the chorus and I thought at one time I would soon be fit for a lunatic asylum. I was anxious to try and see how I should have to manage when I have my twelve but I think I shall send them for my friends to adopt. Your share will be a pair of twins. Mr. Borden is to stay here all night. He always asks how the deaf girl is when I see him. He can't get over that joke. Mrs. Stevens is well but is stormed in, so she can't get out of the canyon only by walking across hills as parts of the road are washed away.

February 6, 1878

Ruf, Father, Mr. Levy, Mr. Fleming and Joe Hatch went to Pescadero this morning to have a railroad meeting. They will stay there all night so I am here with Ma and Lil. Mr. Borden came in awhile to talk this evening. He will go back to the Redwoods in the morning.

February 7, 1878

Send a moss picture to Mrs. Capt Spangue in San Francisco. She used to be Mary Brown and has only been married a short time. I intend the picture for a wedding gift. Alvin and I slept here last night in the room where he was born. Father and Ruf got home at five o'clock so Ma made us stay to tea. Weather threatening rain.

February 8, 1878

Wrote three letters after my work was done this morning and sent for a piece of music called "Strawberries and Cream."[23] It has an engraving of a saucerful of strawberries and sugar and cream on them. Real inviting and natural. Father, Ma and Lil were here to supper and we had a pleasant time. I'll tell you what we had just to tease you a little. Fried ham cut thin with lots of gravy, boiled mealy potatoes, fried eggs, hot slaw, cornbread, (good) cup of tea and bread pudding with wine sauce. In the evening we had an entertainment of gymnastics by Master A. S. Hatch in which he lifts the spoon holder over his head and does not let it fall. Wonderful performance.

February 9, 1878

After Saturday work was done, I went to the

---

[23] Strawberries and Cream: a march by Charles Kinkel, published 1868.

milliner and got a new common hat, brown straw trimmed with black velvet. Got also some fresh candy and oranges. When I came back Fannie was here with her crochet to sit an hour or two and chat. Clarence nearly shocked him to death by clasping his hands around Alvin's neck. Poor child, he could not cry and I just happened to look that way in time. I shall be afraid to let them go out of my sight after this. Spent the evening at Ma's and came home in the rain at 1/2 eight.

February 10, 1878

Went to Church twice today. Alvin was so good this morning that I ventured out this evening accompanied by Ruf and Lil. This morning the girls in the choir behaved so rude and laughed so much. Mr. Gaffney was obliged to address them. I guess they felt cheap. One of the young men in the choir is a minister's son and he kept passing around the hat and writing notes during service. This evening the text was, "The battle is not ours but God's." Coming home we were caught in a shower. I forgot to say all our family, Deacon Hatch and wife and Deacon Knapp and wife and a number of others walked down to the beach in the afternoon. We carried Alvin down by turns but he walked back. The ocean was beautiful and calm. We got several nice shells.

February 11, 1878

Nothing but rain today and just as dismal as can be. I have hardly done anything, it was so dark and lonely. Ruf had to work in the shop all day helping with a wagon.

February 12, 1878

Ruf, Father and others went to Purissima today on Railroad matters and did not get home till dark. Wesley's wife and three children came over to spend the day and take lunch and supper. I had a jolly time I tell you with the racket and when night came I felt as if I had been washing or scrubbing all day. I was so tired of the noise. Alvin of course tried to make as much racket as the rest and I was nearly crazy.

February 13, 1878

Nothing but rain today, so I kept busy with my needle. I would sew till I was tired, then crochet to rest myself, then read a story from "Peterson's magazine."

February 14, 1878

Railroad and rain are the topics of conversation here at the present time. Ruf goes downtown and stays awhile, then comes home to tell me Railroad news. I do hope we can have one here. It would make times so much better and land so much more valuable. But it is hard to tell when it will come, neither you nor I may live to see it.

February 15, 1878

I think I am getting slighted. Valentine's Day and "nary" one. I guess my beaux are throwing off on me. Yesterday was the day but I thought they had forgotten it and would be sure to send them today. That is what I get for being married. I might have got a few if I had been single.

February 16, 1878

It is just a week tomorrow since I have been out to air my hat so I thought I would go down to see Ma rain or shine and sure enough we had to come home in a hard rain but it only took a few minutes to get here and was not worthwhile staying down to the hotel all night for the wind is blowing hard and looks as if it had set in for a good rain.

February 17, 1878

I guess I went to church twice last Sunday because I knew it would rain and keep me at home today. It just poured and the bell did not ring so there was no Sabbath School or Church service today. I spent the time quietly reading on the sofa as I did not feel very bright.

February 18, 1878

It still continues to rain. Ruf, Mr. S. Walker, Mr. Doble, Mr. Marston and others were obliged to go to San Francisco on R.R. business and do not know but what they may go to Sacramento before they get back home. I hated to have Ruf go in the rain, but it could not be helped. Alvin and I went down to Father's to stay till Ruf returns. It rained so hard I put on a pair of Ruf's boots and tied my dress up in a stylish way out of the mud.

February 19, 1878

Terrible rain and wind, it blew down one of Father's gum trees and almost broke out two tall cedars at the side gate. Wesley went up to fix them.

February 20, 1878

It cleared off a little this morning and I went home and built a big fire in the kitchen to dry the house. Cleaned my birds and did several things then came back here. Ma and I sleep together and Father and Alvin sleep together so we have a cozy time. Alvin does not wake at night and father thinks it's such a treat to have a baby in bed. I suppose it reminds him of the time when we were babies.

February 21, 1878

Got three letters, one from Clara, one from Lizzie and one from Mary Brown. All contained good news as all were in perfect spirits at the time of writing. Clara is very busy about her Fair work and I wish her success I am sure. I intend to go over if I can travel the muddy roads in March. Ruf came on the noon stage so we are in our own little room tonight. He reading and I writing. Alvin calling for "faver" to come to bed with him, poor little fellow. While I was away from home I made a new black basque[24] and it looks real neat. I must retire now as it is ten o'clock.

February 22, 1878

Washington's Birthday and the most beautiful day of this year, regular summer weather. Ma came up here this morning and declared I should not stay in the house but should go to walk with her and afterward take lunch at the Hotel as Ruf was away on business.

February 23, 1878

Ruf was up to the Redwoods yesterday and is almost discouraged at the state of things up there. The last rain raised the creek so high that it carried off a great quantity of last year's lumber that was piled on

---

[24] Basque: a Victorian fashion which refers to a closely fitted bodice or jacket extending past the waistline over the hips.

the edge of the creek. A large tree also blew down striking against the mill in its way, breaking the smoke stack and crushing most of the floor of the Saw Mill in. Altogether the damage is over two thousand dollars. Mrs. Stevens and husband were obliged to leave their house as one side of it blew in and they slept in the ox barn nearly scared to death before morning.

February 24, 1878

Went to Church and Alvin slept during service. The lady who plays the organ got offended at the Choir so there was no playing and nobody to start the hymns and it was a complete failure. On the part of the singers, I think I will try to play for awhile but my trouble is, I forget to pump half the time and it sounds as if the music was dying with consumption. The text was 84th Psalm, 4th verse. Did not go this eve as I was afraid to come home in the dark and Ruf had two gentlemen to entertain besides Alvin and could not go with me.

February 25, 1878

Another fine day. It makes me feel like another person to see the sunshine again. I have had two callers today and have been very busy also making fancy cake for tomorrow will be Ma's birthday and I have invited the family to dinner here. I have made a nice gold cake and frosted it, also a lot of small Silver cakes for dinner corn starch in cups etc. Alvin has been playing outdoors most of the day.

February 26, 1878

Oh, what a shame it is to think I had expected the family here today and it is pouring rain so that I can't start a fire in the kitchen at all. We were obliged to cook breakfast in the sitting room and Ma is sick today too on her birthday. Well I shall have to bear the disappointment I suppose.

February 27, 1878

It rained today pretty hard but more in showers so that, with the aid of an umbrella, Ma and Lil came up at three o'clock. We had dinner at five. I know you are anxious to know what I cooked so I'll tell you. A large fat duck roasted, mashed potatoes and turnips, boiled onions, pickled beets, fresh bread, butter made this morning, tea, preserved pears and cake. We all enjoyed our afternoon and evening very much. They got caught in the rain going home.

February 28, 1878

Ruf went with Mr. Levy today to collect some money so I sent for Ma to come and help me pick the remains of the cold duck. We just had a cold lunch with a hot cup of tea to wash it down and we had lots of fun over our "Carcass" lunch as we termed it. In the afternoon I went down with Ma and practiced on the piano for two hours.

March 1, 1878

Just as I was doing my work this morning, a strange lady called to ask if I could play in Church on the organ. I thought that was all the business she had to attend to but behold she kept sitting for three mortal hours. From nine to twelve. I felt like telling her to go a dozen times for her conversation was about her family affairs and about every one else that she ever knew, till I almost went crazy. I suppose she thought as she had a patient listener it would be well to air her long list of troubles. She talked so fast and steady that I could not get a word in but was contented to nod my head once in a while when she looked my way. Poor little Alvin was really talked "to sleep." He was sitting on the floor eating oranges and fell asleep. After she went away I had to hurry my lunch and then do my work in the afternoon. Protect me from any more such visitors I say.

March 2, 1878

I guess I will have to go to school again in order to learn how many days there are in a month or perhaps you will be kind enough to help me. Did not do much today but embroider a little and walk around outside with Alvin. It was too pleasant to stay in the house. In the evening we went to rehearsal for Sunday. Fannie Freitas will play in the evening and I will try to murder the music in the morning. You may be sure I picked out old hymns for the first performance.

March 3, 1878

Rain, rain all the time. I had my hymns practiced but did not go as there was no service in the morning, but we went in the evening through all the mud and succeeded very well. I took the tunes "Hebrow." "Martillo" and "Laban"[25] and managed to play better than I expected to and the singing was very good. Ruf held Alvin during service and once he said "Mama sing," but I didn't hear it.

March 4, 1878

Alvin is 21 months old today. I wish it was 21 years. No I don't because then I would be an old woman and I don't care to be so old yet. It has not rained much today but I really believe we are to have too much of a good thing this year.

---

[25] Lowell Mason (1792-1872) was a leading figure in 19th century American church music. He composed over 1600 hymn tunes. His best known works include "Joy to the World," "Nearer, my God, to Thee," and "Mary had a Little Lamb."

March 5, 1878

Ruf went to the Redwoods today. The cook has left up there and Mrs. Stevens was cooking for the men till Ruf could get a new cook. I wrote a few lines down, had supper late and must now go down to the hotel to help with the ball supper.

March 6, 1878

Last night was a grand time with the Masquerades. Father gave the supper and had about sixty to eat. I helped set and wait on table. We went to bed three o'clock this morning and slept till eight. Woke and found it raining for a change, so that we were not able to get home till ten o'clock. The masquerade was not as select as the last have been, there were too many who acted rough, too many men dressed in women's clothes and too many women in men's clothes. I didn't like it. I did not go in costume.

March 7, 1878

I made two cream cakes this morning and other cooking at noon. Lizzie Messerl came from San Francisco. She intends to go to school here for a couple of months. She has had but little chance to study and is glad of the opportunity to learn. She will help me with the work before and after school. It is raining real hard and the roads are in a terrible condition.

March 8, 1878

Lizzie and I hurried with our work then took a walk to the hotel. Lizzie staid with Alvin while I went to call on Mrs. Compton a lady who has been quite sick for three weeks. She has a young baby and has taken cold which settled in her kidneys making her disease very painful. I think of sitting up tonight with her.

March 9, 1878

I feel pretty tired tonight. Lizzie and I took up the kitchen matting and scrubbed the floor. Picked bouquets and cleaned the windows, birds etc. Besides I sat up with the sick lady till two o'clock in the morning. Fannie Freitas and I were together for company so I have had but a short sleep and Ma and Lil wanted me to go with them to call on Mrs. Davids. We did and got home a little after nine. Now I will do my hair up and tumble into bed as soon as possible.

March 10, 1878

Went to church this morning. Text was Matthew thirteenth chapter, eighteenth verse. After a short lesson on it he read the rules of the M.E. Church which are very strict. He got pretty warm in his discourse when he spoke of having Fish ponds and grab bags at the faire. He said that it was only a game of chance, but I don't agree with him. I think in this way, we give ten cents for a fish and most always get something worth our money, besides the money is going for the Church. I played Hymn's "Martyn, Siloam and Guide." Got along first rate, will go this evening if it does not rain.

March 11, 1878

A very nice day. I went over to the school with Lizzie this morning and she seems to be pleased with the teacher. She says the little boys stare at her terribly but she pretends not to notice them. I advised her to pay attention to her books and not notice the children. Jennie McGinty and Mrs. Perry called.

March 12, 1878

Made pudding and sponge cake besides baking bread this morning. Wrote a letter to Clara telling her I would not be able to come to Redwood on account of bad roads though I feel very much disappointed about it. Ma sent her a nice piece of moss work to sell at the fair. Maggie Walker called and gave me an interesting account of a chase she had with a cow. She hardly knew whether the cow was after her or she after the cow.

March 13, 1878

Just as I was going out to call on the Minister's

wife Mrs. Freitas and baby and Mrs. Perry and baby called. As I noticed that each of the ladies had their crochet with them, I pretended that I was ready to sit down and sew although I was in a fidget all the time, for, I had taken special pains crimping my hair.

March 14, 1878

Wrote a letter to Clara also one to Cousin Mary. Lizzie is getting along nicely at school. She gets home at four o'clock and helps to get supper. Went down to the hotel to practice the hymns for Sunday. I chose "Cast Thy Burden on the Lord" for a voluntary. It is real hard and will require much practicing.

March 15, 1878

I believe Clara holds her fair tonight for the benefit of the Mission. And I hope her class will be able to win the banner this year. Weather beautiful.

March 16, 1878

Ma invited us to spend the afternoon and take supper with her today. We did so and had a splendid time and a good supper of chicken with blackberry pudding. We came home after Ruf got out from Lodge. Forgot to say I sat up with a sick lady last night accompanied by Mrs. Nichols, so I am fearful sleeping now.

March 17, 1878

St. Patrick's Day comes on Sunday this year, but it has been very quiet here. I read in the "Evangel" that St. Patrick was not a Catholic, he was also born in Scotland, but of Irish parents. Some of the Catholics wouldn't swallow that I know. Went to church this morning, played my hymns right and got along nicely with the choir. The text was from Psalm 119, verse 167. "I have gone astray like a lost sheep." It rained this morning so we had no preaching.

March 18, 1878

The third anniversary (no, I mistake the second as we have been married three years today) of our wedding. I asked Ruf a few days ago how we should celebrate the day and he said we could get Ma to have a turkey dinner for us and then we could start for the City, put up at a hotel and pretend we were just married. Now that is all very fine and I should enjoy it but how would it sound to have "Auntie's sweet boy" calling Mama? I am afraid it would not look bride-y; however Ruf had sudden business that called him to San Francisco on this noon and Ma had arranged a pleasant surprise for us. She invited us to take lunch with her which we did and behold she had a fine repast prepared in honor of the day. Cold meats, lobster salad, (so good that I was ashamed of the quantity I ate) baked potatoes, preserved blackberry mince pie, iced cake and a cup of chocolate. Beside this she has a large cake ornamented especially for us and she insisted on my taking it home. I wish I could send a piece to you. Ruf went right away after lunch and I do not expect him back till tomorrow night. Our married life has been so happy that one can scarcely realize that we have spent three years together.

March 19, 1878

Hurried with my work this morning and went down to the hotel to sit a while as I was alone. Lizzie had fire made and supper cooking when I got back. Ma and father came up in the evening fearing I would be lonesome as Ruf had not got home but he came before they went home at eight o'clock. I had a nice meat pie for him all hot and he enjoyed it very much. He brought five pairs of stockings for Alvin, two prs of white, 1 pr pink and blue stripe, 1 pr red and blue and 1 pr navy blue. I am afraid the pink will fade but shall be careful with them.

March 20, 1878

Nothing happened today. I made cake and cleaned my house a little then sat down and mended my week's clothes. Alvin amused himself most of the time with a cigar box and a rope to it which his mama calls a wagon and it serves the same purpose.

March 21, 1878

Mr. Borden came from the Mill today. He says the roads are getting better. I went to Fannie's to rehearse the Voluntary for Sunday. I chose, "Jesus Lover of my Soul," as sung by the choir at Redwood. I think it so pretty. Got a letter from Clara Shelley. Lil is to sit up tonight with Mrs. Compton, the sick lady.

March 22, 1878

Ruf went to the Mill this morning and will not return till tomorrow night. I made some choice cookies. Here is recipe:

1 1/2 cups white sugar
1/3 cup sweet milk
two eggs
1 cup butter
2 teaspoons cream tartar
1 teaspoon soda
1/2 teaspoon nutmeg and flour to roll.

They are nice. I put a little milk on the tops of them just before putting into the oven to make them shine. I had my oven too hot and burnt a dripping pan full. When I burn anything Ruf always says, "Never mind, it is good for the stomach ache."

(No flour? Did she forget to include it?)

March 23, 1878

Did some ironing of starched clothes this morning.

Father bought some marbles for Alvin and he is crazy over them. He has them in his wagon, then in his pocket and then in his hands and jumps around like a wild Indian. I suppose I'll have a good chance to mend pockets after this. Lil, Lizzie, Alvin and I are the occupants of the house tonight. We look like three old maids and an adopted nephew. Received the paper "Leisure Hour" with two beautiful chromos of the Easter Cross. Also "Cricket on the Hearth," with two chromos[26] of children playing.

March 24, 1878

Went to church this morning. The weather was rather cloudy but we hoped to find the sun shining when we came out of church. Instead of that it was pouring down rain and I had to borrow an umbrella from the minister in order to shelter Alvin and my new hat. Ruf was very thoughtful and met us halfway so he carried Alvin the rest of the way home. I brought a library book called "Ernest Richmond and his Little Mother." It is splendid and I sat up till eleven o'clock to finish it. Tells how a child converted his father. Read it if it is in your library. So stormy we have no service this evening.

---

[26] Chromophotography (chromo) is a technique somewhere between painting and photography which evolved in the second half of the 19th century.

March 25, 1878

Rather a pleasant day after the rain. Ruf is laying out the garden and I went to help him but found the ground too damp for my feet especially as there is a large hole on one side to let the air in. It looks like a bay window on the side. Must mend Ruf's coat now.

March 26, 1878

After cleaning the house up a little I went out to help Ruf in the garden. We laid out two large rings and made four parts to each with paths between. While Ruf planted things in the center I laid out the border with primroses and daisies. It is tiresome work I tell you. Alvin tried to help me by pulling up and tramping on the flowers as soon as I got them nicely finished. But then you will say, "A little help is better than none, especially from Auntie's sweet boy."

March 27, 1878

Rec a letter from Clara also answered one from Matilda Hauss today. Lizzie is very much interested in her studies and I help her every evening to do her sums and find her geography lesson on the map. Father, Ma and Lil were here to dinner. Had stewed chicken, potatoes, corn, cake, preserved pineapple and floating islands. Ma was not feeling well, had a pain in her back.

March 28, 1878

Did my housework and helped Ruf lay out some flowerbeds this morning. Called on Mrs. Gafney this afternoon.

March 29, 1878

Went over to the school this afternoon. There was speaking and singing by the large boys and girls. Everything passed off in a fine manner. Some of the pieces were excellent. It rained hard when school was dismissed and I was obliged to carry Alvin home in the rain. Fortunately I had but a short distance to run.

March 31, 1878

We expected the presiding Elder today but sickness prevented his coming. The collection however was taken up for his benefit. Alvin did not behave very well in Church today. He sits beside me and when I play the organ he wants to put his fingers on the keys. He was better this evening because Ruf had him in the back of the Church.

April 1, 1878

Well I did get nicely fooled this morning. Mr. Borden was here and told me that Ruf had been calling me for some time out at the gate. So I ran out and when I could not see him I went to the stable and all around the place till I was out of breath. Then Mr. Borden told me I need not look any longer as he guessed Ruf had gone on a fool's errand also.

April 2, 1878

Ruf and I went to spend the evening with Mrs. Metzgar who lives 1/2 mile from here. We had a pleasant time. On our way home Ruf stepped in a pond of water and wet to his knee. I laughed all the way home but I won't laugh when I have to clean the mud off tomorrow.

April 3, 1878

The ladies met to make preparations for a Sunday School concert as the library needs new books. Mrs. Gaffney, Mrs. Johnson, Mrs. Freitas and myself are appointed a committee to train the children. There is work ahead for us I know and my hands will be about full with the choir meeting too.

April 4, 1878

Fannie Freitas spent the afternoon here. She was making a new dress for Clarence, blue and white calico trimmed with blue chambre. Very neat and we thought it would be nice to have one for Alvin like it and with white sun bonnets they would look like twins at the Odd Fellows picnic. So Ruf got the calico this evening and I have cut the dress out and got it half done. Lizzie is to have review in her studies tomorrow and I heard her spell three hundred words just now, she missed 84.

April 5, 1878

Went to rehearsal this evening. I have two new tunes to play for Sunday. One is in a minor key and I don't like it so I shall have to practice it well. The weather is beautiful and we have a new moon.

April 6, 1878

Worked hard scrubbing and polishing, sweeping, dusting, arranging bouquets etc. till 1 o'clock. Then worked in the garden till after three. Dressed and went down to the Hotel. Ruf went to the Mill this morning and when he came back Ma made us stay to tea at the hotel. I was glad of it for I felt too tired to cook.

April 7, 1878

A lovely day. Went to church. The sermon was to the children and the church was full. We played hymns from "Fresh Laurels." The text was Matt 7th chap, 17th verse. "Every good tree bringeth forth good fruit and a corrupt tree, evil fruit." Mr. Gafney made it very interesting for children and parents also. In the eve, when services were half through, a drunken man stumbled in and sat down beside a lady. She felt so bad she did not know what to do, but he leaned his head on the back of the pew in front and went to sleep. Just as Mr. G. was praying the fellow began to snore and I am afraid the prayer did not reach the ears of many there. While we sang the last hymn he was coughing and vomiting and the worthy Deacon Hatch was about to show him the door.

April 8, 1878

Windy today and no news to tell. In fact I see that I shall have to shorten some of my stories or I will take up too much room and come out wrong in the end of the book.

April 9, 1878

Ruf went up to the Mill to sow grain on the top of the hills and I do not expect him back for a few days. Weather still rather windy.

April 10, 1878

Dreadful windy today. We went to the church to practice with the children for the S. S. Concert they think of having Apr. 21st.

April 11, 1878

Thursday and just as windy as can be. My starched clothes nearly blew to pieces before they got dry. I went down to see Ma awhile in the afternoon and played over my hymns for next Sunday. I chose Mear, Rockingham and Siloam, with the chant, "Thy word is a lamp unto my feet," for a voluntary.

April 12, 1878

Sewed in the morning and at three o'clock went to help the children practice. Mrs. Gafney, Mrs. Johnson, Mrs. Freitas and Mrs. Rufus Hatch are the committee. In the evening we had rehearsal for church on Sunday. We are to have a new member of the choir, the new teacher is a young man named Chauncy Dunn.

April 13, 1878

Saturday always brings lots of work so Lizzie and I have been very busy. Ruf did not come home from the Mill till quite late and we had to make butter, bread and cake this morning besides our sweeping etc. Father and Ma came up in the evening bringing some nice ripe bananas with them.

April 14, 1878

Went to church in the morning. We had an excellent sermon to parents. Mr. Gafney says many mothers want to know at what time to begin to punish their children and he says that when they are still too young to walk but will struggle in your arms in anger then is the time to clasp your arm around it strongly and let the child know it has a power stronger than its own to battle against.

April 15, 1878

Another rainy day. I guess it will be a benefit to the crops for I heard Ruf say the ground was already beginning to get very dry. I planted some flower seeds a few days ago and I hope they will turn out well. I laid out several nice shaped beds and planted Candy Tuft, Larkspur, Lady Slipper, Pansy, Lobelia, Portulaca, Morning Glory, Scarlet Runner, and Sweet Peas. If you would like some seeds next year perhaps I can furnish you with them.

April 16, 1878

Quite a pleasant day. I have not done much of anything today. Fannie and Clarence were here all afternoon. I have taken cold and am afraid I shall not be able to assist in singing very much.

April 17, 1878

We met again to practice for our concert. We have some good pieces and some good speakers but more that are too stupid for anything. I have most of the playing to do as Fannie sings alto and it is hard to play soprano and sing alto. I was too hoarse to sing at all today and they could hardly get along for the little ones had depended on me so much in some of their pieces.

April 18, 1878

Ruf went to Colma today to attend a Railroad meeting. He started at five o'clock and got back at eight at night. He went in his buggy as far as San Mateo and took the cars for Colma. I have been busy with the children for we intend to have the concert next Sunday eve.

April 19, 1878

Went down to the Hotel to play my morning hymns.

Chose "Retreat, Guide and Dennis," in the afternoons. We practiced at the Church again. One dear little girl six years old speaks a piece called "My Brother." It is so cunning, I'll tell you how it goes.

Who is it picked up all the chips
Who strewed the floor with kite and whips
And in the wash tub sailed his ships
My Brother

Who was it ate the currant jell
Who threw my kitten in the well
And made me promise not to tell
My Brother

Who is it a tiny mustache does wear
And oils and combs it with great care
And in the middle parts his hair
My Brother

Who is it that I love the best
Of all the boys both east and west
Although he is a perfect pest
My Brother

April 20, 1878

Saturday with its work as usual. Then I cut some flowers for the wreaths and prepared the cross for the girls. Ruf painted it yesterday. We are to have ten large girls for Christian Graces: Patience, Virtue, Hope, Love, Knowledge, Faith, Charity, Experience, Godliness and Temperance. It is very pretty. Three strong voices sing the verses and the girls go in one by one. Patience holds the cross and Faith and Hope each hang a wreath on the arms of the cross. Temperance twines some lilies around the cross and Knowledge hangs a basket of fruit on the cross. Charity kneels before the cross till told to rise, then all sing a verse. First part of it they take hold of hands and form a circle, then they sing. "Now we part, but these remaineth, Faith and Hope and Charity." As they sing that, all step back leaning. Hope and Faith on each side of the cross and Charity in front. It is beautiful. I plan for the singing and intend to help sing if my cold is better. I would like to explain the whole of the exercises to you but they are rather lengthy.

April 21, 1878

Attended Church this morning as usual and in the evening we had the Concert. All the exercises were interesting and everything passed off nicely. We collected about $15.00 for S.S. papers and the children deserve great praise for doing their part so well. Nice moonlight to come home in.

April 22, 1878

Have done but little today. Cut out some sewing in the afternoon.

April 23, 1878

Planted some pansies seeds this morning and pulled some weeds from my garden. The Lady Slippers are beginning to stick their heads up and the Candy Tuft is doing well. Took a nap in the afternoon while Alvin was asleep.

April 24, 1878

After my morning duties were over I went down to the Hotel as Ruf was in the city today. I spent the afternoon there and Lil came back and slept with me at night. Alvin is as cunning as ever.

April 25, 1878

Lizzie brought "Little Women" from the school library and I have enjoyed reading it very much. The school gives a holiday tomorrow so that all may attend the picnic.

April 26, 1878

Went to the Odd Fellows picnic today at Hatch's Grove. Had a very pleasant time, did not dance but looked on. Ruf took me in the buggy as is generally the case. Some folks began to spread their lunch as soon as they got on the grounds. Ma did not go neither did Lizzie because she had nothing to wear. Went to rehearsal.

April 27, 1878

Saturday again. Dear me, how often that day makes its appearance with scrub, wash window, cooking, blacking the stove etc. but finally when night comes, although it finds us tired, we have a look of content on our faces as if we knew the house was clean anyhow and bouquets picked for Sunday.

April 28, 1878

Went to church in the morning but was obliged to remain home in the evening on account of toothache. I hurt my tooth while I was eating supper and I really thought I should go crazy before night. Ruf put a hot brick to my face and wet a towel with pure ammonia which took the skin off in a place as large as a silver dollar. He finally had to go to the Doctor and get some medicine which was so powerful that it had to be applied with a brush to the gums. But I was relieved very soon and feel much better.

April 29, 1878

Lizzie did not go to school today. She intends to go to work now and so I have engaged her to work for me and she washed today. It blew terrible but we managed to get part of the things dry and left the rest in soak.

April 30, 1878

I helped Lizzie hang up the clothes this morning and to iron a few things. Then went down to help Ma with her tables as she expects to have a ball supper there tomorrow night and generally prepares the castor bottle, cleans the spoons and forks and a good many other things that will help for tomorrow.

May 1, 1878

There was a picnic in the Grove and a ball in the evening at Pacific Hall. Lizzie went with a young man and staid till three o'clock. Ruf was door keeper for father at supper time and I poured out tea and coffee while the others waited on table. There was about 75 to supper and all seemed to be satisfied. We came home at two o'clock a.m.

May 2, 1878

Feel quite sleepy after the ball. Lizzie does not seem to feel bad after her night of dissipation[27] and Lil came to see me this afternoon as gay as a lark. So I guess age is beginning to tell on me and I can't stand as much as I used to.

---

[27] Dissipation: the adjective dissipated is used to describe people who've lost their moral center, and instead of following the rules of conventional morals, preferred to be utterly self indulgent.

May 3, 1878

Made a nightgown today and cut out some pillowcases and sheets for Alvin's bed. I intend to tuck them and put tatting on the best ones. My plants are growing nicely I have one Saint Joseph's Lily up and some Larkspur and mignonette.

May 4, 1878

Yes, it is possible that scrub day has arrived again but I only took a light share in the work today for Lizzie thought she could get along without much help. I gathered several nice bouquets as we have an abundance of roses now.

May 5, 1878

Played the organ as usual but I intend to give it up after today as I got a letter from Lizzie Anderson wanting me to come and visit her this week and also one from Clara stating that her father would be absent a few days and hoping to have me with her during the time. Ruf says I may go so I do not think it worth while for me to take the work of playing the organ as long as they have another lady to take my place.

May 6, 1878

Lizzie is washing today and the wind is blowing

very hard so I am afraid the clothes will not look very white. I starched for her but I'm not able to wring much. I intend to leave home on Wednesday.

May 7, 1878

Ironing took up most of the day. I packed up a few things to take with me tomorrow. My tooth has been aching very bad and I will have it taken out as soon as possible.

May 8, 1878

Left home this morning at eleven o'clock with Ruf in the buggy. The ride was splendid over the mountain. I took the two thirty train for San Francisco and arrived here in good order, baby baggage and all. Lizzie Anderson was delighted to see us. Captain was at home but intends to sail for Mendocino tomorrow. I am pretty tired tonight after so long a ride.

May 9, 1878

Went downtown this morning and had my tooth extracted, but not without pain. On the contrary, I suffered a great deal for the points of the prongs broke and stayed in the jaw. I fainted but soon got over it. Left Alvin with the children.

May 10, 1878

Lizzie and I went shopping all the morning. I bought sheeting pillow case muslin and a number of other articles amounting to $17.00 dollars. Lizzie bought some brown linen for a suit. Got home hungry and ate strawberries.

May 11, 1878

Mr. Hanson, Lizzie, Alvin and myself went to San Lorenzo today. We went over on the Oakland boat, then took cars for Brooklyn, then a livery team to San Lorenzo. I enjoyed the trip as I have never been there before. We did not get back to the city till eight o'clock.

May 12, 1878

Oh, what a lot of bells are ringing today. So unlike our quiet little village where we only expect to hear the bells of the Methodist and Catholic Churches. I wanted real bad to attend service at the Metropolitan Temple but somehow I find it more difficult to do as I wish when away from home. Breakfast is late, baby needs more care or something. It was a relief however to find the streets less noisy for I almost go wild with the racket and wish myself back in the country.

May 13, 1878

Came to Redwood today; found Clara as well as ever and as usual was greeted with a broad grin. I declare my mouth is tired already from laughing and goodness knows how wide it will be stretched before I leave this Asylum (lunatic) for Clara and I are both noted idiots when left half an hour in each others company. We had beans for dinner.

May 14, 1878

Clara and I called on Mrs. Snow this afternoon. While there, a man came with strawberries for sale. Clara bought a box of them and we had a feast of them when we got back home. I must not forget to tell about our fun last night. We made a nice little bed for Alvin on two chairs and he slept well. But this morning we found that the mosquitoes had bitten his face considerably. So I intend to salt him tonight. Clara and I lay awake till after eleven talking about the lecture on Temperance given by Mr. Sheppard and we were comparing notes.

May 15, 1878

Had lots of fun last night. After we had prepared ourselves for bed we discovered that a mosquito had prepared himself for a midnight serenade and I was not particular about listening to his musical voice. I armed myself with a broom and wet towel, turned up the gas and began to hunt for him. I wore a short night dress and must have looked very comical especially when I jumped up on the bed and struck at him. Clara called me captain of the Mulligan guards.

May 16, 1878

Left Redwood this afternoon. Had a tiresome ride over the mountain but got home right side up after all. I hated to leave Clara for we have a splendid time and enjoyed every minute of our time together. Last evening we intended to be extra good so we sat down to read poems from some of the best writers, but it was no use. I could not make that girl behave herself. Of course I was putting on my most dignified air (being a married woman) and chose a piece suitable, it was about a man who thought his wife was small and it ran thus- "My wife's a winsome, wee thing" now she aught not to laugh at that. Then she read about an old maid (I might have known she would have that subject on her mind.) Thus sits she etc. I tried to find beauty and sentiment in the piece but failed to do so and to make her think that I appreciated her fine delivery I kind of smiled at her. I imagine I hear her silvery laugh now. Thank goodness my mouth can come back to its natural shape again now.

May 17, 1878

Lizzie kept house very well while I was away and I found everything in order on my return. We had a great deal to do today trying to straighten up the house and get the baking done for tomorrow so that we can go to the May picnic. Ruf is at the Freemasons lodge this evening. Alvin has been talking about "Wedwood City" and "Aunty Lalar" all day.

May 18, 1878

Had a pleasant time today. The school gave a picnic and they did well. The children marched from the school house at ten o'clock while the band played "Floral March," and when they reached the grove, they formed a circle on the dance hall and sang "Tis Merry May." They then crowned Laura Rock as Queen of May and her maids of honor addressed her, etc. They then twined red, white and blue ribbons around the Maypole while the band played "Captain Jinks." They had several other exercises and marches, finally forming an arch with sticks and the Queen passing under the arch followed by her minister and maids of honor. They then sang "Away to the Woods, Away." Ruf took me over to the grounds in the buggy and I was glad I went for I had not thought of going till this morning. Lizzie enjoyed herself too.

May 19, 1878

Did not go out at all today. Lizzie and Lil went to Church this morning. Mr. Charles Walker came back with Lizzie as the night was so dark she was afraid as a drunken man had made his appearance at Church and been put out for acting rude. He got up during prayer and told Mr. Gafney to go to _____.

May 20, 1878

Wash day and lots of clothes as I had some dirty from my trip and the picnic and Alvin had so many stockings, panties and aprons but Lizzie rubbed hard and I rinsed and hung up for her. It was a dull day and scarcely anything got dry. We are both pretty tired tonight.

May 21, 1878

Ironing, starching and this is soup day and we did have good vegetable soup with dumplings in it. Ruf got home from the mill at six o'clock and said the supper tasted so good. We had mashed potatoes and young turnip greens too but soup fills up so quick.

May 22, 1878

Lizzie and I took a nice ride today. We went to Purissima, then almost to Amesport Landing, then down to the beach and back. We were gone all the afternoon. Lizzie and Alvin seem to enjoy the ride very much. The day was pleasant and the roads not very dusty.

May 23, 1878

I asked Alvin to open the door just now and he said, "I tan't." And this morning when he hurt his finger he said, "Doodness Dacious." I am afraid if Aunt Clara heard him she would hug him and nearly smother him with kisses. There is to be a sheet and pillowcase party at the Hotel tonight and I am going as a spectator.

May 24, 1878

Nice weather today. Lil brought her sewing and we enjoyed a nice chat together on the porch. I feel sleepy after sitting up so late last night. It was a funny site to see so many phantoms

May 25, 1878

Lots of housework today but I took a light share in it as Lizzie was more able to do it than I. Ruf is so fond of custard pie that I made one and then had crust enough left for a peach pie. Both were good. I must give Alvin a bath now as it is getting late and Ruf will soon be home from the Lodge.

May 26, 1878

Went to church this morning. Alvin fell asleep on my lap and Mr. Gaffney made such a noise that he frightened the poor child terribly. I looked up for I really thought he had gone crazy but I guess he only got warmed up. Mrs. James Hatch played the organ and I squeaked out a little tune to help along. I've been reading all afternoon.

May 27, 1878

Another wash day, it does seem as if washing makes everybody out of humor. At any rate I was in bad spirits and I had to rinse and starch an awful pile of clothes. I feel better now than it is over and everything looks nice and clean.

May 28, 1878

I went down to see Ma today and she made me stay to lunch. Then I came home and made a pretty flannel shawl for somebody's twin and Lizzie did the ironing alone. It has been very windy today.

May 29, 1878

Took a nice ride with Ruf today. We went to the ranch to see about the colts. One of them stepped in a squirrel hole and is very lame now. I saw Jennie Mc Ginty. Alvin wanted to drive the horse coming home.

May 30, 1878

Wesley's wife sent for me this morning as she did not feel very well and I stayed with her. I sent Phoebe for the doctor and my mother and at nine o'clock a baby girl was born. Just the sweetest darling you ever saw. A sweet little face, lots of black hair and as fat as a dumpling. I did wish it was mine. She is feeling first rate at present. Her mother came at noon on the stage. This is the second time I have been with her and both times since Alvin was born, her other baby is only 20 months old.

May 31, 1878

This is Father's birthday. Lil gave him a bottle of pomade and box of shaving cream and I gave him a pair of handsome suspenders, stone color, embroidered with blue silk with steel buckles. He was pleased with them. Ruf went to the Mill this morning and did not expect to get back till tomorrow but he came home tonight quite late after supper was cleared away as I had to fix up some dainty dishes for him.

June 1, 1878

Made bread and butter this morning, then went to work and mixed up a lot of donuts out of the buttermilk and as all good things come at once, a man came around with nice ripe currants and he offered them cheap so I took five boxes. Lizzie and I put them up in bottles. I had 11 quart jars when done. So our Saturday has had many variations. I am awful tired. Gave Alvin a bath and curled my hair.

June 2, 1878

Went to Church and heard a sermon on Barrooms. It happened that a new Saloon opened on the corner near the Church today and a free lunch is given to all. Of course an Irishman keeps the place as it is to be called "The Shamrock." Lizzie went to church this evening and Ruf stayed at home with me. Alvin has been performing for us.

June 3, 1878

Washing all day. We are having a nice large kitchen build and suppose we will have plenty of room to stir around in when it is finished. Ruf went to the Mill this evening and Lil is going to sleep with me tonight.

June 4, 1878

Alvin is two years old today. It hardly seems possible that I am mother to a two years old boy. He can count ten without a single mistake and can talk so plain that people think him older though his size is not large for his age. I took him down to the hotel and father gave him a bag of candy. I got him a small comb for his hair.

June 5, 1878

Ruf is at the Mill and I do not expect to see him till Saturday night. Mrs. Gaffney, Fannie Freitas and Lil were here this afternoon. Lizzie was sewing on a nightgown, I was making a little wrapper and Fannie was making some calico aprons for Clarence. Our tongues rattled and we enjoyed our social very much. Lil stayed to supper the rest went home at five o'clock.

June 6, 1878

Lizzie has an invitation to the Minstrels this evening and I think I shall go also as I need a good laugh not having a good grin since I left Clara four weeks ago. We did quite a lot of sewing today. I basted and Lizzie ran the machine.

June 7, 1878

Went to hear the minstrels last night. Did not get home till near twelve. Charlie Walker came home with Lizzie and Lil escorted me. I had Alvin to carry and felt pretty tired when I reached our gate for he is very heavy especially for me. I did not love the performance at all and some of the things were so silly it vexed me to listen to them. I thought Alvin would be delighted, but instead of that he was very much frightened and turned pale when he saw the black men with banjos. I will retire early tonight.

June 8, 1878

Ruf came home this evening at 8 o'clock. He was obliged to walk down from the Mill and of course was very tired when he reached home. But he had to go to Lodge as he holds office at present. I gave Alvin a bath and now he is sleeping soundly in his crib.

June 9, 1878

Did not go to Church today. A lady named Mrs. Souther played the organ in the morning and Fannie played in the evening. The singing was quite good, so Lizzie says, Mrs. Davids came to call this afternoon.

June 10, 1878

Washing today and the carpenter busy building the new kitchen. Ruf digging in the garden and Mr. Nichols white washing the fence. So it has seemed a real busy day all around. Mrs. Nichols called in the afternoon to ask me to make cakes for the Festival that is to be on Wednesday.

June 11, 1878

Mr. S took our kitchen chimney down today, stove etc. Lizzie took the bread over to Ellen's to bake it. I kept out in the front garden with Alvin and watered the flowers. Ruf helped to build the new chimney and we were able to cook supper on our own stove. The kitchen is splendid and I have a nice large dresser in one corner.

June 12, 1878

Ironing and cleaning up all day. It seems as if everything was covered with smut. And I have washed my hands dozens of times today. We are going to the Strawberry Festival tonight so I will have to get ready. We made two cream cakes for the festival.

June 13, 1878

We had a splendid time last night. We did not

leave till twelve o'clock. I had Alvin dressed very pretty in a blouse, and he kept awake till eleven o'clock. I was almost afraid he would get sick for everybody gave him candy and nuts to eat. I helped the ladies pick a basketful of strawberries. Mrs. Souther sang some beautiful songs and a young lady named Lucy sang also and played some opera pieces on the piano. The evening passed pleasantly $30 was cleared. Ma came up awhile this evening.

June 14, 1878

Went over to the school this afternoon as it was closing day and (they) had an exhibition. Many fine pieces were spoken and songs sung. The scholars have improved very much since Mr. Brooks became principal. When I came home Lizzie had taken the dining room matting up and turned it so that it looks like new again Mr. Holloway came around with currants and I bought several boxes and Lizzie and I made quite a lot of jelly. It looks as if it would be very good. Lil has just come to stay all night so I will close.

June 15, 1878

Alvin and I went up to the Mill for Ruf today. I took Ma's horse Fannie, she is so gentle I was not afraid to drive her. I had the seat all to myself and sat Alvin on a pillow at my feet. I got along nicely as he sat still and talked about the flowers that grew on the roadside. Ruf was glad to see us. We ate dinner in the cookhouse and started for home at five o'clock. Ruf drove and I enjoyed the ride very much. Lizzie had supper ready when I got home and a splendid strawberry shortcake for dessert.

June 16, 1878

Received a letter from Lizzie Anderson with some nice embroidery for pillow slips. Ruf went back to the Mill this afternoon so as to be there early Monday morning as he is sawyer he is obliged to be on hand. Lizzie and Lil went to church and Ma and Father came up to stay with me till their return. I was glad to have them as I should have been very lonely.

June 17, 1878

The carpenter did not work on our new kitchen today so we have plenty of room to do the washing and Lizzie was done quite early in the afternoon. Had ham, potatoes and greens for supper. Our vegetable garden is looking fine and we will soon have more than we can use.

June 18, 1878

Fannie came up and brought her sewing this afternoon and we had a very pleasant time chatting together. Lizzie was ironing and baking all day. Father took Alvin out to ride a little while. I have just begun to read "Infelice" by, Augusta Evans Wilson,[28] the one who wrote "St. Elmo." Got a letter from Clara today. She is lonesome and wishes I was there to trouble her again. Besides she says the "skeeters" are pretty bad and Alvin would keep them from biting her. I pity the poor things if they have to depend on her tough hide for a supper.

June 19, 1878

Mr. Borden was down today, says things are going lively at the Mill. I got a letter from Ruf's sister, she is preparing to come out to California to live. Her son and daughter are living in Los Angeles and they think of going there too. Lizzie and I sewed steady all day. I basted and she ran the machine. We made four sheets, six pillowcases and two bureau covers. Had delicious vegetable soup for supper.

June 20, 1878

I wrote two letters this morning and three this afternoon, so I have been occupied as one of the letters held six pages closely written and each of the others had four pages. Named our calf Blossom, how do you like it? Missy has gone to rehearsal for Sunday.

---

[28] Augusta Evans Wilson or Augusta Jane Evans was an American author of southern literature and a patriot of the south. She was the first woman to earn $100,000 through her writing.

June 21, 1878

Ma made me a present of a beautiful singer today, he is just a ball of gold and a sweet singer. I have not decided what to name him yet but think of calling him "Cherry." I ought to copy you and name him Moody,[29] Sankey,[30] or Philip Phillips,[31] after good singers. Sewed considerable today then Ma, Lil and I went to make calls. We struck the wrong day for almost everybody was on a picnic to the redwoods. So we left our cards under the doors and after finding one lady at home we finished our calls and hastened homeward. I must now take a bath and retire.

June 22, 1878

Ruf came home very late this evening. Fannie Freitas and Clarence were here to supper. Got a letter from my Uncle in Seneca Falls, he wrote that Cousin Mary was nearly blind. It seems that she got cold in her eyes and the doctor thought it was scrofula[32] and experimented on her eyes till she could not see when a light was brought into the room. My uncle has taken her to Syracuse to have an oculist attend her.

---

[29] Dwight L. Moody, (1837-1899) was an evangelist and publisher.
[30] Ira David Sankey, an American gospel singer and composer, known for his long association with Dwight L. Moody.
[31] Philip Phillips was commonly known as the "Singing Pilgrim."
[32] Scrofula or mycobacterial cervical lymphadenitis is often associated with tuberculosis.

June 23, 1878

Lizzie and Lil went to Church this evening and as Ruf was gone too I was just beginning to feel lonesome when Ma came in to stay until the girls came back. Alvin did not take a nap today so he went to bed early.

June 24, 1878

Busy day as usual. Put up some strawberries for winter. Lizzie has been washing all day and has just gone to bed with a headache. Lil sleeps with me every night while Ruf is away. I suppose I'll have her up in the night going down town for assistance after a while.

June 25, 1878

I hired two boys to weed the beets. I gave one seventy five cents per day and the other who was too lazy to move I gave fifty cents. He made me awful mad, if he saw me watching he would work first rate, but as soon as I was out of sight he would lean against the fence and sit down on the wheelbarrow. Ruf told me to get somebody to weed and lay out my flower garden and I will try to get a Chinaman for a few days.

June 26, 1878

I went down to the washhouse last evening to get a man but they would not come for one dollar. So I was telling Wesley and as he has left the Hotel to go into other business, he agreed to come and work three days for me. I told him I would just as leave have him around the house as a Chinaman.

June 27, 1878

Wesley cleared the walks of the gardens and laid out several nice flower beds. He also made a walk with bottles for borders. My candy tuft is a very pretty flower, it is crimson and looks just like velvet.

June 28, 1878

I worked some with Wesley in the garden this morning. Used the hoe till I blistered my hand, then I pulled weeds for a change. In the afternoon Lizzie and I went down to the hotel to supper and to spend the evening. There is a nice lady and her daughter boarding there now. Their names are Cross. We spent a pleasant evening. Lizzie showed us a new game played with a key. In fact she mesmerized most of us. One person leaves the room and the others hide the key where the absent one does not know. She is then lead into the room by two ladies who put their hands upon her shoulders and she will walk directly to the key or follow it if another person walks about with it in her hand.

June 29, 1878

Alvin and I went up to the Mill in the buggy today and brought Ruf home with us. The day was very warm and I almost smothered going up the canyon. We got terribly sunburnt. Stopped at Mrs. Bowman's ranch a few minutes and got some cherries. Got home after eight o'clock and found supper nearly spoiled waiting.

June 30, 1878

Ma and Lil came up this afternoon. We are having quite warm weather for the coast but won't brag because we will be sure to be greeted with fog if we do. Lizzy is at Church. Alvin is playing.

July 1, 1878

Everybody is preparing for the fourth and there has been a number of boys around selling flags today. I bought two large ones and a dozen small ones. We intend to take Alvin's rubber ball and stick it full of flags and ribbons then hang it on the porch in front, and let it swing and turn around. I think it will look quite pretty.

July 2, 1878

Lizzie and I went to the stores this evening. I bought fifty cents worth of cherries, plums and bananas. Then we went to Mr. Levy's and bought some red, white and blue ribbons and a pair of cunning ankle ties for "Auntie's sweet boy." He does look so cute in them. I intend to dress him in white with tri color sash and bows, red and white striped stockings and his ties, straw hat with red, white and blue band.

July 3, 1878

Ruf came home tonight so as to be here tomorrow,

we are all invited out to dine with Ma. There is to be a picnic at the "Grove." Lizzy is making great preparations to go with a new dress etc. Received a letter from Minn. today, very bad news. Ruf's brother in law, Jesse Hanford, is dead. He started East about two weeks ago and was taken sick on the cars and died after he had been in Minn. a week. This sickness was pneumonia. Also got three other letters. One from Lizzie Anderson, one from Ruf's sister, Eunice and one from Martha. I must give Alvin a bath and do my hair up fine for the 4th.

July 4, - July 22, 1878

Well I hardly know where to begin for I have been playing sick so long I scarcely know what to say for myself. I suppose you know I did not go down home for my Fourth of July dinner but I celebrated the day far different. I thought as Ruf was home we might as well call in a few friends, and I would play Circus for their amusement. So to make a long story short about seven o'clock in the morning a sweet fat little baby girl came to spend the fourth with us and we decided not to leave home but to remain and entertain her the best way possible. Since then I have been kept in my room till a couple of days ago. I am allowed to dress and sit in the other room by a cozy fire. I am getting along nicely and mean to take good care of myself. Ruf would not run the saw mill for over a week, so that I would not worry about him being away. My friends have named the baby Columbia Independence and Martha Washington, but they are such long names. I think I shall call her after sister, Lillie Edna Hatch. I will call her Edna, not Lil. We are all pleased with a girl but I do not intend to spoil her any more than I did her brother, Alvin. He says, "Mines baby," and is delighted with her.

July 23, 1878

Tuesday and ironing. I am not allowed to be mistress of my own house yet, so I play nurse all the time. I wash and dress the babies and dose the tiny one with catnip, saffron or peppermint tea and occasionally a dose of gin for the colic.

July 24, 1878

Nurse has gone out to see a sick lady so I will write a few lines. Baby was dreadful cross last night and although I did not have to take care of her I fell worried and could not sleep while she cried, so I intend to lie down and take a nap if I can.

July 25, 1878

Baby is three weeks old today. Lizzie Anderson, her husband, mother and two children came to visit Ma for a few days. They got here at one o'clock, drove clear from the city. I was delighted to see Lizzie and expect she will be here most of the time as we always have so much to talk about.

July 26, 1878

"All quiet on the Potomac," that means baby is asleep after squalling nearly all night with colic because her precious Mama ate a large saucer of blackberries and baby got the benefit. Lizzie and her mother were here to lunch. They talk of going to Pescadero tomorrow as a large party are going from the Hotel and Ma will go with them.

July 27, 1878

It seems very quiet here today. All the folks gone to Pescadero and my nurse gone away too. I had quite a time giving baby a bath but Lizzie helped me.

July 28, 1878

Ruf came home about eight o'clock last night and the party from the Pebble Beach came about the same time. They broke down about two miles this side of Pescadero and were obliged to hire a team from the livery stable to bring them back. I guess they had too many pebbles aboard. Capt., Lizzie, her mother and the children ate supper with us tonight.

July 29, 1878

Baby rested very well last night. Lil slept with me and every time baby would stir (for her dinner) Lil would say, "Shall I heat the gin," and she would be asleep the next minute. It was too comical to hear her. Capt. Anderson carried baby down to the Hotel for me today and I walked down and stayed all the afternoon. I took a ride about four o'clock and it gave me an appetite. I feel better for being out and intend to take a short walk each day. "Auntie's sweet boy" is very cunning now. He talks so nice.

July 30, 1878

Lizzie has been ironing all day. I sewed all the afternoon, baby is good now. Fannie Freitas was here this evening. I must now undress Alvin and prepare for bed. Lil is here. Capt. and family went home today. I miss them very much, it will be lonely for a few days now.

July 31, 1878

Sewed in the morning and after dinner took the children down to see Fannie. Stayed a couple of hours then came home and read. Received two letters, one from Uncle telling me that Cousin Mary is better. Her eyes are getting so that she can see a little. The other letter was from Mrs. Todd.

August 1, 1878

Babies are well. Little Edna sleeps all night and nearly all day so that I have plenty of time to rest. I have been quite busy with my recipe book today. I have written off a number of new ones besides pasting a great many that I cut from the "Vermont Journal." Weather is foggy in the morning and clear toward night. Hotel is full of boarders at present.

August 2, 1878

Today is baking day. We made pies, cakes and bread, all of them turned out well. Babies are well. Ruf thinks of going to the city to meet his sister and her husband. We got a letter telling us that they intended to start about the first of Aug.

August 3, 1878

Saturday's work and other things take up the day. Baby has had the colic nearly all day too and I have been obliged to keep her in my arms most of the day.

August 4, 1878

Edna is one month old today and is very fat. She weighs 13 lbs. and is quite a bundle to carry. By the time I get the shawl on her she seems to weigh a ton to me because I don't feel able to carry her. Weather is quite warm and pleasant.

August 5, 1878

Lizzie and Ben Griffith went to Church last night. I intend to go in the mornings as soon as baby is old enough to leave.

August 6, 1878

It seems to me that ironing day is always a warm day and we have nearly melted today. Lizzie ironed most all day. Edna makes quite a wash and a good deal of fancy ironing for such a little baby.

August 7, 1878

Ruf is away at the Mill but will be home after this week is ended and will then drive up once or twice a week. Then I'll have more chance to ride out.

August 8, 1878

I have been quite busy sewing as I sent to the City for some goods and do not believe I shall feel contented till every stitch is finished. I have pink calico at twelve cts per yd to make a wrapper. Do you like it? I think it looks like a checkerboard. I am to have a narrow ruffle down the front and Spanish flounce in the back. I sent for two dozen white pearl buttons to go down the front.

August 9, 1878

Made a cake today from a new recipe and as I found it very good I will write it for you.

One cupful white sugar
Scant half cup of butter
Half cup sweet milk
1 1/2 cupfull of flour
Two small eggs
1 teaspoon cream tartar
Half teaspoon soda
Flavor with lemon extract

Stir the flour in slowly, pour into a cake tin lined with buttered paper and sprinkle a little powdered sugar on the top before baking. For a large cake twice the quantity is nice.

August 10, 1878

As this is Saturday there has been little done except cleaning and I suppose you can guess just how that is done so I will not weary you with it. The man from the city was here with fruit so I bought six boxes of blackberries to preserve. They are nice large ones and have a fine flavor. Speaking of preserving reminds me of a joke I saw last evening in the paper. An old lady having heard about preserved autumn leaves put up a few jars of them, but when she went to eat them she declared, "They wasn't worth the sugar that she wasted on them."

August 11, 1878

Managed to go to Church this morning after leaving baby comfortable. Alvin and I got there in time for the voluntary. The sermon consisted of a description of the missionaries' work, their number of Churches in different countries and the number of persons attending meetings. It was quite interesting to some, but dry to others as I noticed several taking a nap, among them our worthy deacon who is Knapp by name and nap by nature.

August 12, 1878

Ruth took quite a party of us to the Redwoods today. Mrs. Crouse, her daughter Mamie, Lil, Alvin, baby and myself. There was a wagon full, we had a splendid time. The girls gathered ferns and wood moss but I was obliged to stay near the house so as to watch the children.

August 13, 1878

As I was cutting a few curls from the head of "Auntie's sweet boy" I thought you would like a ring out of it. His head is covered with just such rings. Weather pretty foggy. Hope to see sunshine in about a week from now.

August 14, 1878

Went down to see Ma today. She was busy making pies and other things for the table as they have a new cook who doesn't know how to do anything. His piecrust was just like a lump of lead and he hired out for a first class cook. It is discouraging to Ma. She has her hands full of work.

August 15, 1878

Made three pairs of new panties for Alvin which I think a good day's work considering three birdcages to clean, lots of little chores besides baby to pick up so often.

August 16, 1878

I rather guess you do not care for a diary of today's proceedings but I will give it as near correct as possible. Got up, dressed Alvin, washed his face, combed his hair, ate breakfast, took baby up, washed and dressed her, gave her dinner, fed birds, made bed, gave Alvin piece of bread, baby with the colic, gave peppermint, more diapers, more dinner, washed Alvin's dirty hands, picked up things, ate lunch, more baby, more diapers, more colic, more dinner, cut out an apron, put clean stockings on Alvin, baby cries, more dinner, more diapers, more colic, more more.

August 17, 1878

Saturday flies around pretty often. Baby was better today so that I had more time for other work and not so much baby. Capt Anderson, Lizzie and Alvin (her baby) came today to remain a few days. They drove from the City and got here at one o'clock. Lizzie and I will enjoy a good chat. Her mother from Mendocino will be here tomorrow to visit my mother.

August 18, 1878

We spent today very quietly. Lizzie and her mother ate dinner with Ma and the Capt ate with us because we had his favorite soup. So we had our company divided. Ma sent a nice mince pie up for dessert.

August 19, 1878

Capt Anderson, Lizzie, her mother, my mother and two ladies who are boarding at the Hotel drove to Pescadero and back today. They did not have but two hours time on the Pebbly Beach and broke down coming home. I was glad I did not go for I should have been pretty tired with a young baby to carry. (But not like the last trip, too much lunch.)

August 20, 1878

Lizzie and I enjoyed today very much. We crocheted and talked all day. You know just how you and I like that occupation. Baby was pretty good and Alvin played out in the garden most of the time. I was so thankful to have him off enjoying himself that I did not disturb him for a long while and when I went out to see what he was about, behold, he had packed all the abalone shells from around my flowerbeds and made a garden in the backyard to suit himself. He had Ruf's hoe and was so cunning about it that I had to smile. "I working hard Mama. I make you big garden." Such is life.

August 21, 1878

Three canary bird singing as loud as they can, one boy hollering at the top of his voice, one baby screaming with a cramp, one young girl trying to do the work and one Mother almost out of her senses with the noise trying to stop it. I had to separate the birds to make them quiet, give Alvin a big stick of candy to stop him and give baby a dose of peppermint to quiet her. This is a picture of my home this morning. Now at 7 p.m. Edna is asleep, Alvin is building a block fence, birdies are asleep in their swings, Lizzie Anderson and Ruf are conversing about the expense of children's clothes, Capt A has gone to the post office, Lizzy, the young girl here, is reading the "The Pacific Evangel" and I am writing to dear old Clara.

August 22, 1878

Capt A. and family left here this morning at 8 a.m. for San Francisco. We had a nice time together only too short as is always the case with my friend's visits or my visits to them. We have been setting things straight a little today. Ruf went to the Mill again. He will soon be done sawing as orders are not very many for lumber just now.

August 23, 1878

Baking took up most of this morning. Edna took cold some way and cried so hard with cramps in the stomach that Ruf went for the doctor. He gave a simple remedy that gave her ease at once. I ate half a small watermelon last night and think it did not agree with her.

August 24, 1878

Weather gloomy. We have a great deal of foggy weather lately. There are several families at the hotel from Rio Vista. One party has been there sometime. We went down to spend the evening and heard some good singing by two ladies, Mrs. James and Mrs. Ramsey. They sang some very choice selections and then some comic songs to please the gentleman. "Down in a Diving Bell" and "Now Moses You'll Catch It." I was ashamed of my voice after hearing them sing so I would not pipe a note at all.

August 25, 1878

Alvin and I went to church. The sermon was about the strength of Samson. The minister said that Samson served the Lord thirty years and then allowed himself to be led aside by a woman. He said it was just then as it is now, "There was a woman at the bottom of it." Now wasn't that awful and there I sat giving him all my attention. I felt like speaking up and telling him that the men ought to be too strong to allow a woman to advise them in the wrong direction.

August 26, 1878

Nothing but washing today I always get tired wash day for I have more to do. I get breakfast, dress A.S.B.,[33] wash baby, and when she goes to sleep I

---

[33] A.S.B. stands for Auntie's sweet boy.

wash the dishes, then fix the birds and then get dinner and set table. Some of the time with baby in my arms, so I get tired. Good night.

August 27, 1878

Lizzie ironed today. I took the children down to see Ma awhile and stayed there till lunch. Had a good dish of soup, made a pair of pillow slips and tucked them this afternoon. Mrs. Compton came to see me. She is looking first rate again. Fannie Frietas and Clarence are here so often that I do not mention them every time.

August 28, 1878

Got two letters today. One from Mrs. Minnie Stevens and the other from Clara Shelley. I must go to Redwood with baby as soon as she is old enough to travel. Weather pretty bright today.

August 29, 1878

Took my sewing and spent the afternoon with Fannie. Baby slept most of the time and Alvin played out with Clarence on the sand so I had a pleasant chat. I worked on a fancy eating bib for Alvin. Lizzie got a dispatch from her mother and went to the city for a few days. I hardly know how to do without her, it seems as if there is so much to do.

August 30, 1878

I see by looking at the remaining pages in my journal that I shall have to shorten my account each day as I will not have near enough to finish the year.

August 31, 1878

I guess I shall have to limit myself to three lines per day for the month of September so the account will be short and sweet but not so interesting.

September 1, 1878

Did not go to church today. While baby is so young it is hard to get away. Lizzie went this evening and Ruf stayed at home with me. Mr. Gafney, our pastor, talks of leaving us soon.

September 2, 1878

Ruf got a letter telling us that his sister and her husband would be in SF tomorrow, so he is going in to meet them.

September 3, 1878

Ruf left here early this morning with his horse and buggy and will remain in the city till tomorrow morning.

September 4-8, 1878

Edna is two months old today. Ruf and his sister came in the buggy and (Mr. Murdock) her husband came on the stage. I was glad to see them. Mrs.

Murdock is such a pretty old lady about 53 years old I think. She has white hair, not this common gray look but so white that it has turned golden like a child's hair and it is so curly that she cannot keep it straight. Ruf says she has changed a good deal in 14 years. Mr. M is a very pleasant man. He is 59 years old and a good principal. They are very tired as they have been traveling quite steady for three months. They visited their brothers and sisters in Cohoes, Fort Edward and other places of New York. Their house was in Maine but they sold their farm and intend to make California their home.

September 9, 1878

As I have allowed myself but three lines per day, I thought I would make more room by writing in some places the whole page instead of stopping short.

September 10, 11, 12, 1878

We took the wagon this morning and went to the redwoods. Had a splendid time getting ferns and mosses. Then we had a big appetite and ate a good dinner of corn, pork and cabbage and drank all the pure spring water we possibly could. Then I put Alvin and Edna in Mr. Borden's bed and they took a long sleep after which we all walked down the road in search of ferns. Came home the new road and found it rather rough but pleasant on account of change of scenery.

September 13, 1878

Mrs. Murdock knit nearly one whole sock today so this evening we went down to visit Ma. I did not want Mrs. M to sit too steady you see. We had a fine time singing and playing piano.

September 14, 1878

Sold two dozen chickens today, got fourteen cents for them. Ruf laughed at me for he says I sold my laying and will now have to buy eggs. I may but I wanted to sell my old hens while the price was fair for I have about four dozen young pullets that will lay before long.

September 15, 1878

Went to church this morning and played the organ. Mr. and Mrs. Murdock went also and as both of them are good singers, we did very well for a choir. We did not have a sermon but reading of the progress of the Methodist churches. Ruf went in the evening with his sister. I stayed with the babies.

September 16, 17, 1878

Monday washing took the day, Tuesday ironing had full play.

September 18, 1878

Ruf took his sister down to Amesport Landing this morning and father took Mr. Murdock for a ride with him.

September 19, 1878

Mr. M. has been playing ball with Alvin on our side porch all afternoon and I declare it was amusing to watch them. Alvin has become very attached to his uncle Henry.

September 20, 1878

I baked cake and pies this morning and Lizzie made bread and butter. So we have some buttermilk to drink. I bought 50 cents worth of ripe cucumbers for pickles and will leave them in water all night.

September 21, 1878

Mrs. Murdock and I peeled the cucumbers and cut them in slices and laid them in a jar. Then I scalded vinegar, sugar and spices and poured on hot. I am to scald them three times and then put them away for future use.

September 22, 1878

Mr. and Mrs. M. and myself went to church this morning. Heard a good sermon on the duty of Christians. I forgot to say that Auntie's sweet boy went with us and behaved like a little man. When the minister gets anyway noisy and excited, Alvin opens his eyes as wide as can be.

September 23, 1878

Gave out part of my washing because Lizzie did not feel well and Mrs. M. insisted upon washing and I would not allow it. I am chief cook. I gave them ham, eggs, and mush for breakfast. Cold meat, potatoes and pie for dinner and preserved nectarines, hot biscuit and pound cake for tea besides tending my babies.

September 24, 1878

Got a letter from Clara also a package of Decalcomanias[34] from Chicago. So do not be surprised if you see them stuck along here.

September 25, 1878

Our visitors think of leaving us tomorrow. I coaxed them to stay but they cannot. They have been talking all day about the trip from New York here. They say

---

[34] Decalcomania today known as decals.

the scenery is beyond description and everything is grand as they near San Francisco. They got me in the notion to travel and I wish Ruf and I could take a long journey next year. But, there is no prospect of it at present, times are too hard.

September 26, 1878

Ruf took his sister over to San Mateo in the buggy and Mr. Murdock went on the stage. I miss them very much for in two weeks we got used to seeing them about. They will leave San Francisco tomorrow morning and take the steamer "Orizaba"[35] for Santa Barbara. After spending a week there, they intend to sail for Los Angeles where they expect to reside for awhile if the climate agrees with them.

September 27, 1878

Baking and cleaning house took up the day. Of course everything had to be turned about for I had neglected some while my company were here.

September 28, 1878

Sewed most all day. Made some pillow lace for Mrs. M. for Christmas. I will make the pillowcases,

---

[35] Orizaba: one of the first ocean going steamships in commercial service on the west coast of North America, and one of the last side wheelers in regular use.

tuck them and sew the crochet. She has promised me a quilt for baby's bed.

September 29, 1878

Lizzie went to church this morning and she will stay at home with the children while Ruf and I go in the evening.

September 30, 1878

The last day of the month and last end of the page. Washing and slop, slop all day. Blue Monday, no good drying day.

October 1, 1878

Nothing but ironing and sewing today so will not waste paper.

October 2, 1878

I sent a three cent stamp to get my pictures and I got one hundred and ninety of them. Some are very pretty and I ornamented a cup with some. I bet fifty cents with Ruf that one was a man's head and I won it. We had lots of fun.

I think of trying to raise a gift for our pastor for Christmas and I will start around the town tomorrow and ask for two bits of each one.

October 3, 1878

You see what I have been about today. I have stuck these pictures onto almost everything that I come in contact with.

October 4, 1878

Edna is three months old today and just as bald headed as ever. Ruf told me to write to Lizzie Anderson to know if she and her husband will go to the San Jose Fair month and if so we will join them at San Mateo.

October 5, 1878

I have everything ready to start tomorrow for the fair if on. Received a dispatch tonight saying Capt and Lizzie intend to go. 7 PM got a dispatch that they could find nobody to take care of the house and children. So we have given up the idea of going. Money is so scarce that Ruf does not feel much disappointment and I am comforted with a promise to give Clara a flying visit in a few weeks.

October 6, 1878

Had a letter from Lizzie. She and the Capt and baby are coming out next week. I am really glad.

October 7, 1878

Washing and baking and a little of everything as we expect company tomorrow. Alvin and Edna are well and the weather is pleasant so I think nothing will prevent our enjoying a good chat.

October 8, 1878

Got up pretty early and had all the work done and house cleaned up and a splendid dinner waiting but they did not get here till two o'clock. They were detained before they left the city.

October 9, 1878

I must a scratch a few lines to you but I declare I've done nothing but talk today so I won't be able to give a very smart account of myself. All well.

October 10, 1878

Lizzie and I crocheted all day except while we were spanking the children for making too much noise so we could not talk! Lizzie has a very mischievous boy not quite two years old and he got into my closet this morning and broke a large bottle of sweet oil, and I did not find it out till afternoon so you can imagine the condition of my floor with all that oil soaking in it so many hours. I don't know how sweet I've felt toward the child but I do know I hoped his mother would remember to get another bottle of oil.

October 11, 1878

ASB is thoroughly disgusted with his name sake, Alvin Anderson and they had a battle this morning on the front porch in which your boy was beaten. The city lad being stronger shoved him clear off the porch and ASB thought himself killed for a moment. Luckily he struck on a fat place and when he got up he wanted me to kiss it to make it well, but I didn't.

October 12, 1878

Saturday brings work but we made a play day out of it. We all went to the redwoods and stayed all day. Capt, Lizzie and her boy went in their buggy and Ruf, Alvin, baby and I went in our buggy. We came home the new road after a day of pleasure among the big trees.

Ma had a lady come in to pay her a visit today and she intends to stay a week or more. She is Mrs. Merrill of Redwood fame. She came from Berkeley and we were all very glad to see her.

October 13, 1878

Mrs. Merrill and Lil were at church this morning. The sermon was a splendid one preached by Reverend Mr. Jones, our new pastor. Mr. Gafney left last week. The subject was "Blessed is he who not having seen still believeth." It was mostly about doubting Thomas.

October 14, 1878

Capt. and Lizzie left us this morning for their

home and we feel quite lonely. Did not wash today on count of big breakfast and plenty of work.

October 15, 1878

Washing today and a real foggy day too. Besides, just as Lizzie got the clothes out, the line broke and down came the clothes in the dirt. It made her cry.

October 16, 1878

Sewed some and baked some as I have invited Father, Ma and Mrs. M. to dinner tomorrow. We are to have chicken and Ruf is killing it now. Poor thing. (I mean the chicken) and I made a fine cake from a French recipe.

October 17, 1878

Enjoyed today very much as my company were well and seemed to think the dinner pretty good considering the housekeeper and we spent the evening pleasantly.

October 18, 1878

Mrs. Merrill, Ma, Ruf, Alvin, Edna and myself went to the redwoods today you will think we go quite often but you see it is about the only place of resort near here so our guests must go there. Prudence was quite carried away with the place and before she left had made inquiries about everything her eye rested on. "How much do you pay your cook?" "How much do you get a load for your lumber?" etc. We had a good joke with Mr. Borden. I introduced her as a widow Brown and he really thought so and kept calling her Mrs. Brown till I told him. He said it wasn't quite as mean as the deaf girl joke.

October 19, 1878

Have been busy cooking for tomorrow as it is Lil's birthday and I intend to give her a dinner party in honor of her birthday.

October 20, 1878

Although this is Sunday we have no service as I hear that our pastor is absent. I invited Mr. Brooks and Mr. Jackson to dinner with Lil and we had a nice social dinner party. I gave Lil a new linen apron with a ruffle and a new chemise with a cord through the band and window crochet on the edge. She is delighted with them. Mr. Brooks is principal of the school here and he made some smart remarks. Mr. Jackson is a nephew of Mr. Borden and bookkeeper at the Mill.

October 21, 1878

Think of visiting Clara tomorrow so I am all packed (or my satchel is) ready to start. Ruf will take me as far as San Mateo. I will leave Alvin at home and take Edna. I am so nervous I can't hardly wait for morning.

October 22, 1876

A nice warm day. I always like Sunday to be pleasant for it is always so quiet that it seems nice to have it sunny. Mrs. McGinty and Annie went home this afternoon and it seems real quiet without them for we talked a great deal while they were here.

October 25, 1878

Left Redwood this morning and when I arrived at San Mateo I found Ruf waiting for me. We went over to see Mrs. Price and she insisted on my leaving baby with her while Ruf and I drove up to see Mrs. Mahe and the children. She made us promise to be back to dinner with her so I left Edna asleep and we drove up to the Vineyard. Everything looked as natural as when I used to walk the grounds alone or with the children for company. But when we reached the house it seemed as if the very furniture was sad. There was not a happy looking object about the place. Mrs. Mahe looked like a broken hearted woman and Nenette like a woman instead of a girl of 14 years. Gustav was absent and the mother says he feels the loss of his Papa more than the rest do. He was in France when the news of his father's death reached him and he blamed himself entirely for the act that ended his father's life. Gustav says if he had been here his father never would have committed suicide. Madame and Nenette were very much pleased to see me. We spent about two hours with them. Then drove back to Mrs. Price's. Baby had slept well ate dinner and then I had till 3 o'clock to chat. I will leave it with you to guess if we enjoyed our time. I say I leave it with you because you know my weakness, a crochet needle, spool of cotton and some dear old friend to chat with. Then I am happy. We got home a little after five and found supper ready and do you believe it, Alvin did not ask for Mama once while I was away and it is the first time I ever left him overnight. Now that is encouraging. If I want to go again soon, Lizzie is just like a mother.

October 26-31, 1878

Alvin was taken sick with measles the day after I got home so I have been kept pretty busy with him. He is still quite sick but is not having the measles in a dangerous form. I do not think baby will take them. Alvin is very feverish and well covered with blotches. I have not been out and everybody is afraid to come here so I get but little news.

November 1 - 4, 1878

Lil came home on the fourth after nearly 2 weeks of visiting at Berkeley and San Francisco. She says she went with Mrs. Merrill to visit Mrs. Smith in Oakland and enjoyed herself very much. She went riding every day while in the city as captain Anderson has a carriage and horses. She brought a very nice hand glass for a present to me from Mrs. P.V.M. Alvin is not well yet, is quite fretful. Is cutting four double teeth and is not over the measles yet. I cannot leave him to go to church or to run out anywhere.

November 5-9, 1878

Ruf is at the mill for a few days again. They are scaling logs that means taking the measure of them. When he asked me if I knew what it meant I said, "Of course, you are peeling the bark off." Wasn't I stupid or do you think it would have been your answer also? Ma was up here today.

November 10, 1878

Lizzie went to church. Alvin was sick with croup all night so I had but little sleep. Ruf is home till Alvin gets well. Had to call the doctor in, he was so bad this morning.

November 11, 1878

Alvin was so choked up with croup that I was up most of the night putting hot lard and vinegar on his chest and giving him alum and sugar to vomit him. Baby has caught the croup from him and is real croupy too.

November 12, 1878

I made 15 quarts of mince meat today with Lizzie's help. And in fact before I got done with it, I had help from Ma and Lil. They came up to see Alvin and found me peeling apples with him on my lap and they took hold and helped me can it and get it out of the way. Edna is real croupy and I am nearly worn out with Alvin. I have new medicine for his cough and a liniment to rub on his chest.

November 13, 1878

I left Alvin asleep and took baby out in her carriage for a little air this morning. Ruf said that I looked as if I needed air myself after being confined to the house three weeks. It was rather hard for poor little Alvin to get the croup right after the measles.

November 14, 1878

I wrapped Alvin up warm and took him down to the Hotel today. He looks so pale that you would suppose he had been sick three months. He is still very fretful and requires most of my time to attend to him. Edna sits in the high chair and chews on a rubber ring as contented and happy as can be or lies in the crib perfectly willing to let Mama bestow her caresses on her big brother.

November 15, 1878

I received a letter from Iowa and one from Lizzie Anderson today. O' dear, that makes six letters waiting to be answered and I have not found time to sew or write for so long. But the babies are both getting so well that I shall soon have leisure.

November 16, 1878

Received a letter from Clara speaking about her trying to win a prize for writing a book. My advice is "Try, try." I know she is capable of doing well and if her effort is not appreciated don't despair.

Maria Jane Schuyler Hatch

November 17, 1878

Went to church and took Alvin. He behaved nicely and put his ten cent piece into the hat as good as anyone. Lizzie took care of baby for me. Ma and Lil as well as Lizzie will go this evening while Ruf and I stay with the little ones at home.

November 18, 1878

Nothing but work today. Washing and lots of odd jobs to do. I ran down to the store to get some muslin to make a pair of pillowcases for Ma for Christmas present. I sent to the City last week for a very pretty piece of embroidery and I intend to make fine tucks in them.

November 19, 1878

Sewed most all morning. After lunch Ruf took me to ride as far as his ranch and I enjoyed it very much.

November 20, 1878

I took baby in her buggy this morning as far as Mrs. Ames to see her baby. It is a fine boy and just as cunning as can be. I met two of our school teachers on their way to the Hotel to take the stage for San Mateo as school is to close on account of one of the scholars having the scarlet fever.

November 21, 1878

Ma invited Mrs. Davids and myself to tea so I went down there early and spent a very pleasant afternoon. Mrs. Davids was working on a fascinator of red worsted. I must tell you how she was dressed. She looked so pretty today. She is naturally pale and she wore a black cashmere trimmed with silk. At the throat she wore a rushing of white with black lace for a necktie and her only ornaments were coral earrings and breast pin. I admire her taste very much. Alvin and Edna were real good and we had a nice ladies meeting. Lil sewed, Ma, Mrs. D and myself crocheted, Alvin playing blocks and Edna laid on the sofa and kicked up her heels.

November 22, 1878

Fannie Freitas gave Edna a very pretty blue sacque[36] with a white border and she looks so cunning in it that I want to squeeze her all the time. Received a tidy[37] from Clara. It is the prettiest star tidy I ever saw. She is making another for me, the design is a woman knitting a stocking.

November 23, 1878

Ruf got a book called "History of San Mateo County"

---

[36] Sacque was a sack-back gown or robe a la francaise.
[37] A tidy was a fancy covering used to protect the back, arms or headrest of a chair or sofa from wear or soiling.

today. It is nearly full of pictures (lithographs) and some of them are very fine. Ruf paid ten dollars for it. I see the name of John Shelley in several places and see the residence of Mrs. C. Hawes of Redwood.

November 24, 1878

Alvin and I went to church this morning. We had Bible readings. This minister, Mr. Jones, hardly ever preaches a sermon. He generally gives readings from the New Testament. As is the case always some people like him and some do not. He is not as well educated as Mr. Gafney was but he is a good man and I think will do all he can for the people. He is very sociable and tries to get acquainted with all.

November 25, 1878

Washing today. In the afternoon Ruf took me to ride as far as Amesport Landing. I took both children as Lizzie had enough to do at home. Ma and Lil are here this evening.

November 26, 1878

Lizzie ironed and I made Alvin a new coat out of one Lil used to wear. It is a fine piece of cloth $3.00 per yard. The color is between a buff and a pink. I turned it and corded it with brown and put brown buttons on and it is just as sweet as if I had paid six dollars for it.

November 27, 1878

Been cooking all day as I intend to have my family here to dinner tomorrow. Lizzie is cleaning the chickens now.

November 28, 1878

Thanksgiving has been a bright, fine day. The folks came up to dinner and seemed to eat with a relish. I was glad everything tasted so good to them, different from Hotel cooking. Father always seems to enjoy his food so much better up here. This evening we had hickory nuts and apples. Fannie came in to spend the evening as her husband was away and she felt lonesome. Clarence happened to feel uncommon cross. He wanted to fight with Alvin all the time.

November 29, 1878

I ran down to see Ma awhile this afternoon. Of course I had not seen her in such a long time. She was busy filling out an order for 4 dollars worth of moss to be sent to Stockton and another order to New Jersey. So she is doing well with her mosses this year. She has sold about fifty dollars worth and sold thirty five dollars worth of canary birds, her own raising.

Maria Jane Schuyler Hatch

November 30, 1878

Just got word that Fannie F. has a young son born last night. I ran down to see it but it is only a little black headed bundle. She was very much disappointed as she wanted a girl. She intends to call him Ernest Leslie. Clarence does not like the idea and has his nose out of joint.

December 1, 1878

Did not go to church as Ruf was not feeling well. I stayed at home and made it as pleasant as I could for him. Got a letter from Lizzie A. saying she has a box of presents for me and I must send the Express man for them.

December 2, 1878

Washing and open doors today. I always take a fresh cold on wash day. There is so much draught. Alvin played out in the sand all day.

December 3, 1878

Ruf took Alvin and I up to the ranch today and I visited Jeannie (Dolloff) McGinty. I carried a tin pail of mince meat with me and she was pleased with it as she never made any. Jeannie has her house fixed up real cozy with pictures around the walls and fancy articles strewed about.

December 4, 1878

Lizzie and I have been busy nearly all day making two fruit cakes for the holidays. I never tried to make one before but met with success the first time. So if you want the recipe let me know. I had Ruf to crack the almonds while I stoned the raisins. We ate philopena[38] and he caught me before the hour was up, so what shall I make for him.

December 5, 1878

Put two coats of icing on my cakes if that isn't enough I'll put pants on next time. I wish you had a smell of my cakes. You would be anxious to get a bite. I intend to take "Godey's Lady's Book" next year so I sent for it today. Also "Demorest Magazine" for Ma and "Chimney Corner" for father a present.

December 6, 1878

Made Edna a short dress of blue and white opera flannel. It is very pretty and has small pearl buttons down the back. Wesley is having trouble again and has taken his children away to board with a farmer's wife. I am very busy sewing for Phoebe. She was nearly naked for clothes and there was plenty of material in

---

[38] Philopena: a game in which a man and a woman who have shared the twin kernels of a nut each try to claim a gift from the other as a forfeit at their next meeting by fulfilling certain conditions.

the house to make up but her mother neglected to use it. I have cut out three aprons and will sew as fast as I can so that she can look decent.

December 7, 1878

I stayed up till after ten o'clock last night and finished an apron for Phoebe. I do not mean a small one. They are just like making a dress, long and ruffled and have pockets, sleeves etc. I intend another tonight, buttons down the back.

December 8, 1878

I stayed at home this morning and Lizzie went to church as Ruf and I want to go this evening. We had company to dinner (I don't like it for Sunday) Mrs. Simmons and two children and Mr. Borden. Mrs. Simmons has been the music teacher of this place for two years and is going to move away to the City next Saturday.

December 9, 1878

Ruf and I enjoyed the sermon last night very much. It was about the other world and he described it as he imagined it to be, with streets of gold. He then urged us to work and pray. I played all the hymns and had it understood by the pastor that we would sing "One More Days Work for Jesus" for the last hymn but he got mixed up and you can imagine my dismay when he read the hymn "Work for the Night is Coming." Deacon Hatch corrected him and he made an apology saying he knew the piece had "work" in it and perhaps it wouldn't make any difference as both were pretty songs. Mr. Brooks and Lil walked home with us and spent an hour. I must retire as this is wash day.

December 10, 1878

Lizzie ironed and Ruf took babies and myself up to visit Mrs. Markman where my brother has his children. We stayed all day and the little fellows seem to have a grand time playing with Alvin. I took some apples, blocks, candies, nuts and picture books but they cared more for an old cigar box with a string to it for a wagon than all the other things. We came home about five o'clock. Mrs. M. is a woman like Mrs. T. of the Royal Family.

December 11, 1878

I made a white dress for baby and trimmed it with embroidery. I want to put her in short clothes when she is six months old. (January 4th)

December 12, 1878

Received my box of Christmas presents from Lizzie. There was something for each of us. 1/2 dozen linen handkerchiefs for Ruf, two initial handkerchiefs for Ma and two toilet mats, a box of nine pins, a toy watch and chain and a whistle for A.S.B., and a rattle for Edna, a bottle of cologne for Lil, two fine linen handkerchiefs for Lizzie and a glass globe containing a branch of a tree with a hummingbird on it and underneath a tiny nest with three eggs in it. I do believe the eggs are pills. I am delighted with it and a handsome card "Merry Christmas."

December 13, 1878

I went out to buy a few things for presents but got almost discouraged. I finally bought some choice cigars for Ruf and a bookmark of black silk with these words in gold, "The Lord watch between me and thee, when we are absent one from another." I thought it so pretty. I got some stereoscope[39] views for Ma and a woolen skirt and linen check for an apron for Lil. I bought a back comb and Gospel Hymns numbers 1 and 2 for Lizzie.

December 14, 1878

I have thought of going in town before this but Ruf has had some trouble about his ranch rent and we have decided to wait and pay a visit after the holidays. Children are both well. Dr. Dunbar vaccinated Alvin

---

[39] Stereoscopy is a technique for creating or enhancing the illusion of depth in an image by means of stereopsis for binocular vision.

and I hope it will take well. Edna has a ring-worm on the back of her head but I am driving it away with gun powder and vinegar.

December 15, 1878

Went to church and heard some reading from Cor 2. Mrs. Hatch played the organ and we had a good choir. Lizzie and Mr. Ben Griffith went this evening. Mr. Griffith made me a present of a photograph of father's hotel in a nice frame.

December 16, 1878

Ruf had a sheriff's sale today on McGinty ranch. He bought all the cows and horses himself as money is so scarce that nobody offered what they were worth. Ruf hated to sell the things but there was no help for it as Mr. McGinty had served him a very mean trick in having his grain mortgaged so that Ruf could not get any of it to sell for the rest of the place.

December 17, 1878

The weather is getting very cold. I nearly freeze in the mornings when I get up and I have made two heavy cotton flannel petticoats to help keep me warm. Drove up to Mrs. Markman's to engage a turkey for Christmas dinner. Came home and mended socks and Alvin's stockings.

December 18, 1878

We have been married three years and nine months today, time flies. It seems but a short time ago but still I am mother of two sweet children. Lizzie made a popcorn pyramid. I'll tell you how it is done as it is very pretty for a festival table. She takes a large square of stiff white paper and forms a bag such as grocers used before the ready-made ones came in use. Then she trims the large part even as it will stand on a plate. Have the corn popped as even as you can then take white sugar and melt it and dip each piece of corn into the hot sugar then stick it on the pyramid. You can't imagine how pretty it looks. Lizzie is going to make two for the Freemason's supper to be given next week at the Hotel.

December 19, 1878

Mrs. Nichols brought a sweet little sacque for baby as a present. It is the most delicate shade of pink and is made with shell stitch. I think she has done very well for Christmas, two sacques and a rattle.

December 20, 1878

I think of trying to raise a gift for our pastor for Christmas and I will start around the town tomorrow and ask two bits of each one.

December 21, 1878

I collected eight dollars today and I had to walk till I was tired out to get it. Just think, I had to ask thirty two different persons as each gave but two bits. Times are so hard that people did not offer any more than that, even Mr. Gordon when I told him my errand, handed me a quarter.

I was so tired that I could hardly eat any supper and my back aches terribly.

December 22, 1878

Lizzie went to church this morning and I cleaned up the house, gave Alvin a bath and the baby a bath. Then Ruf wanted me to wash his head and comb it with the fine comb and after that, I took a bath and I think I had a regular washing time. Ruf and I will go this evening and Lizzie will take care of the children.

December 23, 1878

Got up early and cooked breakfast while Lizzie washed, then I washed baby and dressed Alvin, swept the floor, washed my dishes and ran out to collect two dollars more. Ruf gave me four bits and Lizzie gave four, so I have now collected enough to make ten dollars. Then I got it changed to a ten dollar piece and have written a note signed by Santa Clause, as I do not wish him to know that I had anything more to do with it than the rest.

December 24, 1878

Edna got a beautiful present by today's mail, it is a large silver napkin ring with her name on it sent from Iowa from a school mate of Ruf's. I was delighted with it. Lizzie put a mask on and went to the parsonage with the note and money I am going down to help Ma with the masquerade supper. Ruf will be door keeper and I will help wait on table.

December 25, 1878

I wish you a merry Christmas Dear Clara, may you live to see many and each one be merrier than the last one. We feel pretty tired after staying up most all night. I receive several presents and will tell you what they are. Lil gave me a China ornament to hold cigars and a watch dog for the, what not. Lizzie gave me a beautiful pair of vases, blue, white and gold to hold grasses on the mantle shelf. Ruf gave me a $20 buggy for Edna (although I got it sometime before Christmas.) Ma calls this Poverty Christmas because she had no money to spare for presents so she made a very handy scrap-bag to hang in the bedroom. It has fifteen different sized pockets and each has a piece of tape sewn on it and the name of the contents written with indelible ink on the tape. Flannel, old linen, strings, patterns, stockings, etc. I think a great deal of it. She also made two picture frames with blue ribbon bows for my room.

December 26, 1878

Alvin got a box of candy from Berkeley. Father, Ma and Lil ate dinner here today. We were too tired to have the C. dinner on the 25th. We had a nice large turkey and things to go with it. Mince pie and fruit cake for dessert.

December 27, 1878

Father and Ruf are both sick with a cold. Ruf laid on the sofa most all day and father had to go to bed in a high fever. Both took cold Ball night as they stood in a draught.

December 28, 1878

Ruf was sick all day but felt compelled to go out this evening to the Lodge as the members intend to give a supper. Ruf being one of the officers cannot very well get anyone to take his place.

December 29, 1878

Alvin was quite sick with his vaccination and four double teeth that he is cutting at once and I did not go out to church at all today. Lizzie went morning and evening.

December 30, 1878

It began to rain this morning early and has been very windy and rainy all day. I made a sweet little hood for Edna of light blue flannel with a narrow piece of white down all around it. She looks cunning in it. Ruf feels better.

December 31, 1878

A.S.B. is feeling well today, he has been making a dreadful racket. We are invited to dine with Father and Ma tomorrow. I intended to make a speech on paper but find that I am rather short of that material and will wish you a happy New Year.

Children of Maria and Rufus

Alvin Schuyler Hatch (1876-1967) Alvin was a respected figure in San Mateo County. He was elected County Supervisor in 1936 and was continuously reelected until his retirement in 1965. He was a member of the Half Moon Bay Elementary School District for 30 years. He helped form the county's first Planning Commission and in 1932 served on the Board of Freeholders that drafted the county charter. He was instrumental in building and improving Coast Highway 1. He also worked tirelessly toward the planning and building of Pillar Point Breakwater.

Lillian Edna Hatch McGovern (Edna) (1878-1964) Edna was very civic minded. On Sunday she played the organ for the Methodist church and often for the Catholic Church when their organist was ill. She was a member of Eastern Star and Daughters of the American Revolution as well as the South San Francisco Women's Club. She was broken hearted when her younger sister, Clara died but remained very close to her brother, Alvin all her life.

Myra Janette Hatch (1880-1899) was committed to Sonoma State Hospital at age five where she died at age 19.

Clara Elizabeth Hatch Kneese (1885-1919) Like Maria, Clara contracted tuberculosis from the family cow. She was very fragile all her life but did marry. She remained very close to Alvin and Edna until her death.

Rest in Heaven

In memory of Mrs. R. H. Hatch who died at
Half Moon Bay, February 20, 1888.

On the brink of the dark flowing river,
    We tarried for many a day,
Waiting the on coming boatman,
    To bear our loved one away.
We watched, with our eyes tear blinded,
    As nearer, still nearer he came,
And we clasped one darling, the chosen,
    As tho' we would argue his claim.

But calmly she watched his coming,
    With vision undimmed by a tear,
She saw past the boatman, a mansion
    Her Savior had gone to prepare.
She saw the bright city celestial,
    The home of the pure and the blest,
And as her feet touched the dark waters,
    She whispered, "In Heaven there's rest."

And our hearts were almost willing,
    When she peacefully glided away,
As we thought of the journey finished,
    Of the painful, the wearisome way.
For we know in that cloudless Home-land
    Where brightest blessings are given,
She has gained at last, the longed for boon,
    Rest, sweet rest, in Heaven.

                                Clara M. Shelley

Acknowledgments

This journal is a wonderful piece of our family history.

We are so fortunate that Maria Jane wrote it. Thank you to family and friends who encouraged my work along the way. Deciphering the journal was a difficult task but a labor of love. We are grateful to Mary Vallejo who kept the journal safe for many years and returned it to me in 1995.

I also wish to thank Violet, Deborah, and Paula for all their help and handholding. You were the perfect team to help a newbie like me publish this book!

Most of all I wish to thank my husband who, years ago, painstakingly photographed each page of the original journal. Without his technological help and superb editing, this project would not have been possible.

Disclaimer

Parts of Maria Jane's journal were very difficult to decipher because of the age of the paper and the quality of the inks used. Most words could be figured out in context, however, surnames were troublesome. If I have misspelled your family name, please contact me at terry.totten@gmail.com and I will gladly make any corrections before the next printing.

www.ingramcontent.com/pod-product-compliance
Lightning Source LLC
Chambersburg PA
CBHW060858120626
46553CB00001B/128